M000278356

LE MÉTIER

LE MÉTIER

the seasons of a professional cyclist

Michael Barry | Camille J McMillan

Third edition 2012

Published by Rouleur Books
An imprint of Bloomsbury Publishing Plc
50 Bedford Square
London WC1B 3DP
www.bloomsbury.com

First and second edition 2010, published by Rouleur Ltd

Copyright © 2010, 2012 Michael Barry and Camille J McMillan

ISBN 978-1-4081-8167-6

All rights reserved. No part of this publication may be reproduced in
any form or by any means – graphic, electronic or mechanical, including
photocopying, recording, taping or information storage and retrieval
systems – without the prior permission in writing of the publishers.

Note
Whilst every effort has been made to ensure that the content of this
book is as technically accurate and as sound as possible, neither the
author nor the publishers can accept responsibility for any injury or
loss sustained as a result of the use of this material.

Michael Barry and Camille J McMillan asserted their rights under the Copyright,
Design and Patents Act, 1988, to be identified as the authors of this work.

A CIP catalogue record for this book is available from the British Library.

Acknowledgements

ALL PHOTOGRAPHY AND ILLUSTRATIONS © **Camille J McMillan**
THIRD EDITION EDITOR **Claire Read**
FIRST AND SECOND EDITION EDITOR **Sofie Andersen**
DESIGN **Jonathan Bacon**
ORIGINAL DESIGN **Justin Greenleaf**
ART DIRECTION **Camille J McMillan**

The logging and manufacturing processes conform
to the environmental regulations of the country of origin.

Typeset in Monotype Grotesque by Rouleur

Printed and bound in China by C&C Offset Ltd

10 9 8 7 6 5 4 3 2 1

Rouleur Limited
1 Luke Street, London
EC2A 4PX

Rouleur

Rouleur magazine is published eight times a year
ISSN 1752-962X
WWW.ROULEUR.CC

For Liam and Ashlin
For Hunter

I would like to thank my wife Dede for inspiring me, for keeping me focused, for encouraging me and for providing a warm calming home. Thanks also for being a wonderful mom to Liam and Ashlin who give me perspective.

  Thanks to my parents, Mike and Clare, for always being on the other end of the line, for listening, for supporting me in pursuing my dreams, and for providing a home where my friends were always welcome. Thank you to Ian Austen for being a thoughtful teacher, editor and friend. Thanks to Brendan Quirk for his support, insight and guidance. Thanks to Guy Andrews, Sofie Andersen and Justin Greenleaf for understanding our vision, for believing in this book and for working on it passionately. Thanks to all of my past and present team-mates for making the good moments richer and the hard moments easier.

Michael Barry

Thank you to Simone, MB and all his team-mates for opening all the doors for me. All in Girona who made it possible, and Justin Greenleaf.

Camille J McMillan

FOREWORD

The snow blew across the mountain road as we ascended. Drivers who usually honked in anger as cyclists slowed their progress now honked at us with encouragement, as our ride had become something extraordinary. "Fresh tracks," Michael said, as we rode the snow-covered gravel road to the Peak-to-Peak highway in Colorado at 9,000 feet. As there were no tracks from anything – short of maybe a deer – on the snowy road that late winter morning, I replied, frozen: "Yeah, because we are the only ones stupid enough to be up here, Barry!" But of course I loved every minute of it too. We warmed up in a café before tearing back down the mountain to reach home as fast as possible. A decade later, I still remember the ride.

Michael has coerced me into training rides that I would never have fathomed were possible. And I am not alone. He has talked me, and our friends, into riding that extra hour, which inevitably becomes two, to see the sights and to push ourselves beyond our comfort level. We'll climb the extra mountain that puts us into snow and freezing digits. But every time I am happy that he has persuaded me to push my limits and experience what I thought was too much.

We have spent countless hours riding side by side on roads that literally nobody had been on yet that day. On our bikes as we rode to extremes, we learned more about each other than in any other setting. Whether training or racing we have shared some memorable moments that matured us.

During an absurdly tough Giro stage in 2005, where we had already done a load of work for our respective teams, we found ourselves dropped from the peloton, together, in the middle of the Dolomites with no other riders in sight. We were into the fourth hour of the race and had 60 kilometres and two mountain passes to go. Despite being destroyed, I started chuckling as we rode together, taking turns in the wind and chasing the peloton. There were close to 200 people in the race that year and of all those people, Michael and I were in no-man's land together. The main group was up ahead and the gruppetto of dropped riders was well behind. Michael asked me what I was laughing about. I responded: "We are alone out here, man. If you told me that we were on the Peak-to-Peak in Colorado, I would believe you." We rode on for hours and, after nearly eight hours of racing, finished the stage, empty but satisfied. The shared experience left a lasting memory.

This book brings me back to every great, mundane and horrible experience that I have had since childhood on or off a bike. It brings back the smells, sounds, and sensations that I try to suppress or relive with every pedal stroke. Michael and Camille have taken all of those experiences that our 'normal' lives have given us and have told the story of the life of a cyclist. They have stripped the glamorous façade from cycling and exposed the life of a professional for what it really is – for better and for worse.

Through failure, triumph and indecision, we persevere. During the hard moments, I have wanted to quit. With persistence and patience, I have plodded on. The trying moments seem to make the good moments richer. This book brings out the emotions that I often have a hard time expressing. The story is one I would want my children to read later in life, so they understand exactly what their dad did before he grew fat.

It's ironic that the sport that keeps me young at heart has buckled me so many times and has more than likely accelerated my ageing, because I still feel like a 23-year-old, although with more responsibility, perspective and humility. Cycling matures us but also keeps us youthful.

Enjoy the book – you'll understand why everyone isn't a professional cyclist but why, for us, it is the best job we could have.

Christian Vande Velde

LE MÉTIER

'Le métier' was one of the phrases I heard often during my first year of racing in France as an amateur. Not speaking French I would focus on words that I heard most often. Along with *putain*, *tant pis* and *chaudière*, *le métier* stood out. What separated *le métier* from the others was that there wasn't a direct translation to English. As it couldn't really be explained, it took me not only that year but also the next few seasons to fully grasp its meaning. The problem was, I didn't really like what it meant once I had finally figured it out.

A foreigner in old world French cycling, I considered myself to be an outsider, from a more modern scientific background where everything was calculated with reason and science to back it up. *'Le métier'* was based on old wives' tales and traditions – remnants of a generation I thought were long gone. Because cycling's icons had done things a certain way, we were expected to do the same, even if they didn't make sense. To me air conditioners weren't evil because they might make you ill, they were what made life bearable in Hong Kong, where I lived as a boy. Wrapping my neck in a scarf whenever it was cold was something my mum would make me do when I was young and something I was proud to have behind me. Putting my legs in the air at every opportunity? Well, that wasn't going to make me a better racer, it was just silly. All these things, and many more, represented what I didn't like about professional cycling.

A decade on, having raced for several French and international professional teams, I have slowly come to appreciate the value of it all. *Le métier* is the sacrifice, savoir-faire, and passion that makes professional cycling different from most other sports as it requires the athlete to give, in virtually every facet of his life. And, amazingly, after being immersed in a world of science and reason, using all sorts of cutting edge technology, and believing in dozens of fads, the things that have stood strong and proved their worth are the elements that make up *le métier*: the traditions, experience and knowledge gained.

When I was younger I loved racing. Whenever I rode my bike it was for one reason alone: to train for races. As I've grown older and matured in professional cycling I have fallen deeper in love with riding my bike. I will always be a pro cyclist, but no longer is cycling just about training and racing. It is now something more profound and will forever be my passion.

What was once the worst time of the year for me is now my favourite; winter is now the time I enjoy most. During the Tour de France, Michael and I discussed how much we were looking forward to our December training rides. It's then we get to meet in the morning and ride our bikes for fun, with an appreciation of our good fortune. We're old pros now, seasoned campaigners. Between us we've raced several thousand times. Yet now that we're so close to the end we want more than ever for it to continue. Perspective, reflection and maturity give us appreciation and understanding. We'll miss *le métier*, and so we treasure it now.

David Millar

WINTER

In bed, lying awake in the darkness, everything from the past and future swirls together to calm or create anxiety. Once the lights have gone out, my mind starts to wander to irrational places as I toss and turn in an attempt to control what I cannot. The preparation for tomorrow's event has been pointed, perfect and professional. Christian Rumeau, my first directeur sportif, would have said: "Il a du métier." I have been devoted. In bed everything converges and then, in a moment, I can accept that the thousands of hours, tens of thousands of kilometres, the diet, my sleep schedule and everything else has been done well. In a race with countless uncontrollable variables it is in bed where I somehow try to rationalise what I will endure and tell myself that I am ready.

Under the covers my leg muscles twitch. They aren't painful but feel full and slightly bloated. The veins that will pulse with blood in the race are now deep under the fluid that my legs retain. I have eaten a feast in anticipation of the required effort and know through experience that I will cross the finish line depleted, as the demands of the race require me to empty my body of every resource. After crossing the finish line, my hands will tremble. Drunk from the effort my sentences will not be cohesive but terse. I will be stripped of every bit of energy I stored during the days prior. The race will have left its mark physically and mentally: my body will be covered in the road dirt that builds up through the six hour race like the soot on a miner's face; my legs will be marked with veins like the roads of France line a Michelin map; my face will tell its own story. Whether we are victorious or defeated, the spectators who line the roads after the finish gaze at us with patience. They see the wear, which I cannot. A cyclist represses the pain, the struggle and the sacrifice.

Awake in bed, it is not the crashes, or even the fierce effort that I fear. We suppress those fears to cope. In the darkness of the hotel room, it is failure that is haunting. Cycling is tactical; the race follows a formula, like a card game. But to play the game well enough to win, the proper resources must be used and the right moment chosen: when to bluff, when to attack, and when to concede. We know our limits and only hope we can somehow push beyond them at the right moment. The moment may only come once in a race that is seven hours or even three weeks long. If we can't push, if we aren't in the right spot at that moment, we fail. What I fear are the tiny variables that make the difference: executing the effort at the ideal moment, and finding a position in the peloton of 200 which swirls like a fierce ebbing river as it speeds along the road. To prepare, we train to adapt to the conditions, the circuit, the environment, the competition, and crashes.

I am trying to sleep in a small hotel in the Italian Alps, anticipating the World Championships. I cannot calm myself. My legs begin to sweat and I twist sideways, the sheet falling to the ground. On the bedside table sits my watch, a bottle of water, a book, magazines, my numbers, a sleeping pill and the course guidebook which outlines everything we are supposed to know about the next day's race but which answers none of the questions that keep me awake. The watch reads 11:30. If my fear of failure and my anticipation of accomplishment persist, I will reach for the pill. In just over nine hours,

I will be lining up for a race that will take nearly seven hours to complete, that will cover 265 kilometres, and that will climb 4,500 metres. From experience I know that the sleeping pill will give my mind and body the rest I need prior to the start.

In an identical short and narrow bed next to mine lies my team-mate and, for tonight, my room-mate. Likely, he is awake as well as his mind cascades through similar thoughts, creating a spectrum of emotions. Tomorrow we will ride the same race but our experiences will be unique. Good legs or bad legs, we will both suffer. In the night we will wake each other briefly as we shuffle to the bathroom, trying to be quiet while finding our way in a dark foreign room cluttered with bags. We learn to find comfort in our rhythmic daily routine as little in our environment remains constant. We move through the seasons, through countries and continents, and from hotel to hotel. Our season, the cyclist's season, seems nearly eternal with only a small break of a few weeks in the autumn. In those few weeks we break the rhythm to breathe outside of the bubble we create and then, progressively, we find our routine again, where nearly everything in our lives becomes focused towards the goal.

I became committed to this goal, to ride my bike as fast as possible, when I first began racing friends around our neighbourhood as a small boy. The environment and the circumstances have changed but the same emotional high and thrill I discovered on my tiny BMX bike remains.

I was born and grew up in Toronto, Canada, where cycling is a fringe sport. First generation European immigrants who were cycling fanatics and understood the intricacies of the sport formed the small cycling community. Most of them raced at a high level in their home country and brought the racing scene to life. They shared their knowledge and experience with the young riders, enthusiastically promoting races and organising group rides, which helped the inexperienced develop their skills.

Toronto is a city of passionate hockey fans, multicultural liberals, and conservative businessmen. The city is known for the long frigid winters, the short hot summers, the swelling suburbs, the towering buildings, the congested roads, the port on Lake Ontario, and the green wooded parks. As a child it was on those roads, in those parks, and between the traffic that I pedalled with fervour, pretending I was in Europe, racing with Coppi or Merckx. Now, the night before the World Championships, I realise I am there, on the stage I once imagined. Maturing through a lifetime spent on a bike, my vision of cycling has changed but still, as I lie in bed the night before the race, I feel the same emotional exhilaration of an unexpected challenge as when I readied myself for the races as a boy. Although cycling is a different sport to what it was midway through the last century, when my childhood idols were racing, the essence of the cyclist remains the same.

Most children live in an imaginary world, and I built mine from the libraries of cycling books that my father, a British immigrant who owned a bike shop in the city, had collected since his youth. The local neighbourhoods and parks became my courses as I coaxed my friends into reenacting the European classics. Having carefully analysed my hero's position, his pedal stroke and his grimace, I mimicked him, even wearing my hat just as he did.

The races didn't end when I reached adolescence. In the winter I rode in snow boots; the fresh fallen snow was a plume of white dust floating up from the wheels, my breath a cloud of condensation in the crisp frozen air, my toes and my hands slowly became numb nubs under the layers of wool and leather. No matter how hard I pedalled, the biting cold pierced the layers and I froze. Yet I persisted because my hero Bernard Hinault had won Liège-Bastogne-Liège, the longest of the northern Classics, under falling snow. On that day, most of the frozen peloton retired from the race, but with the tenacity he'd learned on his family's farm in Brittany, Hinault won. I knew what a cyclist needed to accept to win. In my teens, I found the point where suffering on the bike became pleasure. Pushing myself to physical and mental extremes I arrived home elated. To find the sublime there is a balance where elements of pain and passion become equal: on a bike, pedalling in the environment, a human being can find divinity.

When class was let out early due to falling snow, I jammed my bookbag with my texts and hockey skates. With worn and stretched leather toe straps, removed from my pedals after seasons of use in adverse weather, I strapped my hockey stick to the bike's top tube and rode through the snow. The bike skidded and slid while I danced on it, my weight shifting to keep momentum and balance. It was the same technique as the one I now use as I race across the cobbles in Belgium – one that is learned through errors and experience. A brusque movement breaking the rhythm brings the rider to a crashing halt. The bike should float, the rider's body should be nimble and his mind at ease; tension and fear are disastrous.

Every professional cyclist has developed his technique on the bike in his own unique way. With a common passion and goal, our skills develop in our daily routines and in our contrasting environments from the moment we first stretch a leg over a top tube. Spending hours on a bike every day in Toronto, I slowly evolved into a professional.

On the city streets lined with parked cars trapped by banks of snow, I carefully chose the path of least resistance by following the thin line the car tyres had pressed into the snow, avoiding icy patches and lumpy drifts. In the late afternoon the rows of houses were quiet as their inhabitants worked away in the city centre; the snow muffled distant sounds while those in proximity were acute. The tyres crunched the snow beneath. The build-up of ice on the mudguards made a whirl against the spinning wheels. Although I was in a city of millions, I felt alone in the snow. Things moved slowly. Squirrels that usually darted on the tarmac instead dug and sniffed in the powder for food, their usual panicked demeanour dampened. On the bike I felt at ease, and although it was a route I rode daily, the changed environment transformed the ride into an adventure. Day turned to night on the short ride home. The snow went from stark white to grey as the sun set. In the night's darkness, the snow began to contrast everything it surrounded as it glistened in the moonlight, becoming increasingly crisp under my wheels as the temperature dropped.

Arriving at home, I warmed my frozen toes and fingers with movement and friction. Painfully, blood began to flow, causing a discomfort worse than the frozen sensation that had pained me only moments before. As soon as I was warm and my hands nimble enough to tug on clothes, I stripped off my woolen school uniform and pulled on my cycling clothes. I devoured a slice of bread with honey to get a boost before stomping through the snow to the frozen garage to plug in the electric heater to warm the temperature so that I could ride my bike on the rollers.

In the garage workshop among the hanging bikes, the benches cluttered with tools and punctured tubulars hanging before being mended, I would ride the rollers, listening to music for hours. The first wheel revolutions were uncomfortable since everything – the wheels, rollers, saddle and bartape – was cold and hard. The ice crystals, which turned the windows opaque, would slowly melt, the windows becoming fogged, as my tempo increased and I stripped off my layers of clothing. A puddle of sweat formed between the cylinders as my wheels spun. Unlike a static fixed trainer, which holds the rear wheel in place and requires no balance, rollers develop skill and intuition as the cyclist learns to relax and feel the subtle movement of the bicycle. Riding on top of three rollers is a balancing act, as the cyclist must pedal as if on a road to stay upright yet there is only a foot of spinning surface on which he must manoeuvre. They take the cyclist beyond the effort by also training his cadence and agility. Balancing on the cylinders became innate to me with each passing hour. Without glancing down at my wheels I could sense when I was an inch from riding overboard, repositioning my body and bike before crashing to a halt with the smell of burning rubber filling the small workshop.

Spinning legs turned the cranks, which spun the wheels and turned the cylinders. On the rollers my legs became free and I spun away, relentlessly increasing my tempo until I couldn't spin the whirling machine any faster. There were moments where the ride was a thrill but over hours it felt like tedious work.

The sweat saturating the chamois padding in my shorts began to chafe with the relentless pedalling, eventually opening small cuts on my thighs. My back became sore, as my upper body remained virtually motionless while my legs pumped in circles. In front of me, pinned to the wall, was a poster of my childhood idol Eddy Merckx, on Mont Ventoux in the yellow jersey. For two hours I would stare at the poster while the rollers spun under the rhythm I pedalled, which often spontaneously matched the cadence of the musical beat – I found inspiration in the music and the images floating through my mind.

Now, as a veteran, I return to the rollers when I am lacking the fluidity required to accelerate in a flying peloton. Biomechanically, an adaptation occurs where the body becomes accustomed to the high cadence and begins to flow freely.

As I neared the end of my workout and my thoughts turned to the schoolwork to be done for the following day, my father would come in the garage, his face red from the cold, to hang up his city bike, which he had just ridden home in

Pre-Camp training data, Mallorca

DATE	DURATION	DESCRIPTION	NUTRITION	COMMENTS
04 01 08	120 MIN	Easy rolling	—	—
05 01 08	240 MIN	12 MIN in G²/medio to warm up, search a climb steady for approx 10 KM do 15–20 MIN all out on this climb, another 20–30 MIN of easy climbing in medio @ 70–80 RPM, rest flat and easy 200 W constant	—	—
06 01 08	300 MIN	Climbs: 2x approx 20 MIN in G²/medio, include in these climbs each time 5 MIN at 350 W @ 50–60 RPM, towards the end: 2x10 MIN 300 W @ 110 RPM easy for 15 MIN in between 200 W on the flats	—	—
07 01 08	300 MIN	Flat and smooth, constant approx 220 W, last hour could be less, like sub 200 W but add 6–8 x high cadence for 30 SEC at low power to loosen up	low carbs high protein at dinner	one leg squats 3x 15–20 MIN each leg
08 01 08	240 MIN	In the flat, do 4x4 MIN @ 400 W, easy 4 MIN in between, also 20–30 MIN easy climb at approx 300 W with smooth 70–80 RPM	high carbs	full core strength program +10–15 MIN movement prep
09 01 08	0 MIN	Day off, extra time for your kid and wife, you can go easy for 1–2 HRS for sure, but for me you wouldn't have to	low carbs high protein at dinner	no, day off
10 01 08	300 MIN	Climb total for approx 45 MIN in G²/medio @ 300–320 W @ 70–80 RPM within that, include 3x6–8 MIN @ 360 W @ 50–60 RPM	low carbs high protein at dinner	one leg squats 3x 15–20 MIN each leg
11 01 08	300 MIN	Flat and smooth, constant approx 220 W, last hour could be less, like sub 200 W but add 6–8 x high cadence for 30 SEC at low power to loosen up	low carbs high protein at dinner	full core strength program +10–15 MIN movement prep
12 01 08	180 MIN	Flat and easy, constant 210 W	high carbs	one leg squats 3x 15–20 MIN each leg
13 01 08	300 MIN	In the flat, do 4x4 MIN @ 400 W, easy 4 MIN in between, also 20–30 MIN easy climb at approx 300 W with smooth 70–80 RPM	high carbs	one leg squats 3x 15–20 MIN each leg
14 01 08	240 MIN	Flat and smooth, constant approx 220 W, last 1x10 MIN 320 W @ 110 RPM add 6–8 x high cadence for 30 SEC at low power to loosen up	low carbs high protein at dinner	full core strength program +10–15 MIN movement prep
15 01 08	90 MIN	Easy rolling	high carbs	off
16 01 08	—	Travel day and ergo testing, begin training camp	high carbs	—

the snow and darkness from his shop. He smiled, gave me a pat on the back with his ice cold hands and said: "I'll go put the kettle on." A cup of tea and biscuit after the effort brought comfort, but pushing my body calmed me in a way that allowed me to focus on my schoolwork and enjoy the rest of the evening, and my father's encouragement would drive my passion.

My first pedal strokes were taken before I can remember pushing them out, as I began sitting on a bicycle shortly after learning to walk. I have no memory of the hours spent riding around the house on the tricycle, but the photos my father proudly took document each progression. I began riding a two wheel bicycle at two, racing up and down the cobbled drive at four, and dreaming about the Pyrenees, yellow jerseys and cobble trophies as soon as I saw the images of Eddy Merckx. The heart of that dream keeps me pedalling and pushing.

The photos in the French magazines only showed half of the story. The beauty of the countryside, the champion's arms in the air as he crossed the line and the shining, spinning, silver spoked wheels gave the sport a glamour that only became possible through dedication and determination. Bike racing is also a way of life and not only a finish line, thousands of kilometres or one mountain pass: the pleasure comes with the pain.

With desire, I rode. In the pursuit of a goal and a dream my sacrifice began. Cycling became the priority and overwhelmed relationships, school, and nearly every other aspect of my life. I managed the workload by using every minute I wasn't in school to do my homework, ride or take a short nap. From the early morning to the late evening of my day I tried to maintain balance. Schoolwork was done properly because it was a requisite, a safety net in case cycling didn't turn into a career. Otherwise, my life was focused on the bicycle. Twenty years later, little has changed.

Now I suffer on the bike not only because I still find joy in the effort but because, slowly, it has also become my career. I have obligations to race, contracts to fulfil and a family to care for, yet rarely does the job become a chore. There is comfort in the routine despite the constantly contrasting environments. The cyclist's environment is never static like that of a basketball player or office worker; we aren't confined to a court or a cube. The contrasting environments not only stimulate the cyclist mentally, but also push him to be versatile and resilient: a sprinter must be able to climb and a climber requires speed. A cyclist born in southern Spain must endure the icy northern rain while a Belgian must sweat through the southern sun. Our mental strength is in its elasticity and tenacity – like the physical strength, the mental strength is built while training and racing in contrasting extremes.

During the off season, we grow mentally and physically stronger, as we step out into the cold weather to ride for hours in the rain or snow. Committed to the job and to the goal we ride in conditions that keep most people indoors. In extremes I learn about myself, and my limits.

In the winter, I pedal a steady rhythm labouring over the climbs with my extra weight gained. There is no rush; I am building a foundation as I did as a teenager in the garage and on the snow banked roads. "Miles are like money in the bank," my first coach would tell me. "You want to enter the season with a large account which you will inevitably draw from in each race."

The kilometres pass quickly while riding with friends as we socialise on the bike like the workmen who chat as they dig at the roadside. Winter meals and late nights with too much wine slow us on the bike, but for now, we need these vices to escape from the structure we will soon endure. A cyclist cherishes the moments he has to relax, as they are rare in the midst of a chaotic season. We know that, come March, the job will require unrelenting focus.

Far from Toronto I now live and train in Girona, Spain. Lured there nearly a decade ago by my American team-mates, the small Catalan town is now home. Girona has slowly become populated with foreign professional cyclists who were attracted to the town for its proximity to the mountains, the Mediterranean climate, and the swelling pool of training partners. Riding is easier with companions, especially in the waning months of the season or the damp spring: suffering is easier when you have a friend.

Many of these cyclists' lives are nomadic. They arrive and then leave Girona, following the patterns of the tourists and the migratory birds – in when the weather improves and out when it turns.

Foreign riders cross continents, leaving their families, homes and friends to pursue a dream. It is a gamble. For many, the season is too long and life in a foreign environment challenging – they return home, retire or pursue their career at a lower level. For those who succeed, settle and slowly adapt into a new life abroad, their lives are coloured by the adopted culture. Our lives are simplified when we can accept a new environment and make it our home through the winter. Having two homes on two continents brings a constant feeling of disconnection.

The cycling season ends. As the leaves turn their autumn colours and fall, we are completing our last training rides before a short break from the bike. My training partner, David Millar, already wants to start again where we began our season ten months earlier. During the hundreds of hours we have spent together on our bikes in the damp, chilly winter air, we have developed a fondness for these training sessions. The rides are something we missed during the hectic racing season, and something he is eager to resume despite having just ridden three Grand Tours and dozens of other events. In the winter, riding for hours in the cold, we chat and build our friendship by telling animated stories, discovering new roads and predicting what will come in the next year as we work toward our goals.

As veterans of the peloton, we have tales to tell and experiences to share. Our paths have been similar: from homes abroad, to French cycling clubs, to the professional peloton, we have made similar sacrifices in the same pursuit.

Our bikes are loaded down so that we can endure the winter weather. Weight is rarely a concern when we are training. Durability is of importance, as the bike must resist wear like a workman's boots. Our tyres are thicker and our wheels are heavier. We ride with mudguards to keep the wet road grit from chafing our legs and our crotches. As a child, I rode a similar bike, which was built by my father – now a company pays me to ride its creation.

In the late morning, when the sun is still low but has melted the frost from the road and warmed the air, we meet at a café before we ride. After sipping warm drinks as the business people gather for an espresso and Iberic ham sandwich before work, we recount stories from the previous night, the latest news, and then, after a brief discussion, decide where to ride. Training plans are loose as the races are distant and we decide on a route that will take us to where the weather is best, where the roads are quietest and where we can find what we need: hills, flat roads, or undulating terrain.

Our routes are constantly changing as we piece together roads to make new loops in an attempt to achieve our goals in training while avoiding the mundane or monotonous. Most professional cyclists share the same appreciation of adventure and discovery; we constantly seek new roads and climbs.

The tourists who crowd the streets in the summer, who cheer and yell comments about the Tour de France, are few in the winter months. Like the shopkeepers and students, we are part of the fabric that makes up the town. We roll through the neighbourhoods slowly, wave to familiar faces, and then get to work, pedalling faster, our legs ticking over with the steady rhythm of a metronome as we pass the suburbs and ride into the farmland.

The locals know what we do for a living and what we need to do to prepare for the races. They understand the demands and are respectful. Catalans are private people and rarely approach a champion who they have seen winning on television the previous day. There is sincere respect in Girona, in contrast to the public lives of the cyclists in Belgium, where the tabloids follow their every movement and broadcasters air their failures.

The low winter sun casts long shadows across the drying tarmac as it warms the air and melts the frost from the dormant dirt farm fields. What is alive is vibrant green; the rest is dirty brown. There is a quiet calm that motorists cannot feel; the air is fresh and clean from the night rain and the aromas of earth and spores are pungent. As we climb through the woods, animals rustle the fallen leaves, and the wind blows in calm breaths in contrast to the fierce gale that makes our work difficult in the spring. The dirt in the roadside ditches has been turned by the boars who have spent their night digging for food. In the woods beside the road we will hear the occasional grunt as they scramble through, and in the distance a hunter's rifle fires a few shots. On our bikes we experience the constant changes in the environment that even most of the locals never witness.

The occasional car passes with a touch of the accelerator. The driver toots his horn and waves as he drives to the next town, farm or restaurant. In a moving box he is isolated: the radio wails, the car hums, and the air is

BARRY

- SEAT HEIGHT   80,8
- HANDLEBAR HEIGHT   58,5
-    STEP   13
-    HANDLEBAR   ANATOMIC 46
-    CRANKS   175
-    SADDLE   FLITE TT
- NOSE SADDLE TO   61,2
  CENTER STEP
- SADDLE BEHIND
      BRACKET   11,5

stagnant. The drivers are usually passive towards cyclists but we can sense their haste as they zoom past. A cyclist passing us in the opposite direction smiles and we nod a salute.

David's pedal stroke never appears laborious. Even in the winter months, when his body is unconditioned to riding, he seems at ease. There are few riders in the peloton who spin with such elegance – one of them was the lithe Swiss champion Hugo Koblet who was nicknamed the 'pedaller of charm'. Some are born to ride bikes while others seem unable to find comfort with their upper bodies moving, bobbing and shuffling.

A man on a bicycle is said to be the most efficient means of transportation: it is natural and a cyclist pedalling efficiently and elegantly is beautiful. "Tu as marché comme un avion," a team mechanic told me after a race. You flew like an aeroplane. A cyclist *en forme* appears in flight.

David has a fluidity that eludes most professionals. As a time trial specialist, his torso sits motionless, in a tightly crunched aerodynamic position, while his legs spin like a steam train's piston rods. Despite racing at his threshold with his heart beating near its maximum and his lungs exchanging litres of air every few seconds, he appears comfortable when he races. In that hour he will burn through the energy he has stored in the previous night, due to the fierce effort. Halfway through the race he might stoke his engine with a sugary gel or sweet drink to ensure he can sustain his consistently furious rhythm. Throughout the race, he makes a conscious effort to push beyond the point where his brain tells him to stop – he must. There is burning in his lungs as the air rips in and out and sears his legs as the lactic acid increases. To the observer he seems to be painlessly speeding through the countryside; David pedals with outward charm yet boils internally.

He suffers sleepless nights as his past and his future disturb him. As a 25-year-old, David was suspended from professional cycling for two years due to an admission of doping with the performance enhancing blood booster, EPO. Considered a criminal in France for doping, he spent 48 hours in prison, being questioned as the police searched his house. Within a week he had lost the fortune he had won in his glorious first seasons as a professional. His new Jaguar, his wealth, and his custom home in Biarritz were exchanged for a small flat in Manchester as he sold his possessions to pay the taxman he had tried to evade. Although he was left with nothing but debts, he was liberated internally. David had won many races, a World Championship title, Tour de France stages and yellow jerseys. He had lived his adolescent dreams but the victories had become pyrrhic.

Cyrille Guimard, a directeur sportif who has coached several riders to victories at the Tour de France, predicted Millar would be one of the best ever. He had a "sacré coup de pédale," a saying often reserved for describing the best, which roughly signifies a graceful yet potent pedal stroke. He had the physique to perform and the mentality to win with panache.

David's physique is similar to that of cycling's icons who dominated their generation: Indurain, Merckx, Armstrong. Tall and strong, he is resilient.

Thin and lean, he can climb. With large lungs, he can pump enough air to maintain consistent power during long intense efforts.

Pressured by his peers and influenced by a toxic environment within his team, David eventually gave in and began doping. After being told repeatedly that he could achieve great things with drugs, he accepted. Humans are often weak, as we succumb to moral pitfalls and addictions. Yet, obsession is a vital component in the mentality of most professional cyclists and elite athletes – it gives us the capacity to push ourselves to our physical and mental limit, to reach peak performance. Without the ability to push to nearly abusive extremes, athletes are average; obsessive focus to the point of addiction is a common trait in most of the greatest cyclists.

Cyclists take abnormal risks every day while racing. We fly through blind corners at high speeds, descend treacherously wet mountain roads, and we rub elbows and skirt road signs as we sprint toward the finish line. Our addictive, risk taking personalities allow us to push ourselves to the limit in training and racing to the point of illness in order to reach higher levels of fitness and strength. For a cyclist who risks his life and health frequently, the risk of drug use is perhaps understandable as the reward of victory, fame and fortune tempts. Professional athletes have short careers in comparison to most other professions, as age limits one's ability to perform – knowing the earning years are short, the incentive to maximise compensation is huge.

There are few young cyclists who haven't been manipulated, robbed, and cheated. The sacrifice is great, and when an immature adult is pushed to his limits he will buckle. The generation of riders who rode through the '90s doped to win, to survive in the peloton, and to maintain their jobs as professionals. Cyclists can suffer like few other athletes but to suffer and never feel the satisfaction of one good moment on the bicycle can be crushing. Pushing with every watt of energy the body can exert to hold a wheel in front as riders attack relentlessly, the mind can become weak; we question everything and begin to hate it all, but we persist because cyclists rarely quit. And we rarely quit because the sacrifice has been too great. We hold on to the hope that perhaps, one day, for even only a few kilometres, the opportunity will arise and we will be *en forme* to attack. Even a champion must struggle and persist – with time, cyclists become hardened and accepting.

We couldn't train for hours every day without hope, and even the very best lose far more than they will ever win. On a bicycle you can fly like a plane and the following day crawl like a worm, and we rebound because we can only hope it can't get any worse. But when doping became the norm in the peloton that hope faded for many, and they were faced with few options: to dope, to pray, to accept defeat, or to retire.

Directors, doctors and soigneurs told their riders that to race they needed to be professional and take care of themselves: "Il faut se soigner." Drugs were called *les soins*, which made something wrong seem like a necessity for health. Medicine was not pushed for its performance enhancement but as a way to heal the body from the effort.

Thirteen years ago when I raced my first major international race, the 1996 Olympics in Atlanta, my team-mate and childhood idol Steve Bauer told me: "I am glad I am retiring tomorrow and am not in your shoes. The drugs are potent now." Those words stuck with me, discouraged me, encouraged me, enraged me, frustrated me, and also opened my eyes to the reality of our sport: it had reached a point where no matter how talented a rider was, how much training he did, how fit he was, or how motivated he was, he could not compete with the medicine when the racing reached the extreme. The difference in endurance and power between a doped and clean rider was too significant. Cycling went from sport to black science.

The moment in a person's life when they realise their dream is not reality is maturing in a harrowing way. Naively I thought I could overcome anybody on a bike but knowing the truth, I felt empty. My heroes became ghosts. I had left college, lost friendships, and surrendered my adolescence for my bicycle. Alone in France, distant from my family in Canada, I tried to rationalise my life. The options seemed few: return to school, find a job, or carry on in the hope that things might change.

Living alone in France and racing as an amateur, I matured as I dealt with the challenges. While riding through the Alps I found sanctity. I was forced to reevaluate my motivation in the sport and rediscover the beauty of it. I was 20. With my childhood dreams shattered, I began to dream again.

Every cyclist has a story to tell – some are heroic tales, some of horrifying crashes, and others of drugs and cheating. Most will never speak a word. They accept what has happened, the choices, the good and the bad, and move forward – to survive, our minds have an incredible way of suppressing what we don't want to believe. Millar told his story and found some peace.

As David and I ride side by side we increase our tempo over the climbs. We ride a steady rhythm, not only gauging our efforts by the numbers on our powermeters but also by our sensations; when we feel good we push each other, and when the moment isn't right we ride prudently. Our coaches provide a template for training and with the experience gained during decades of training we now know how hard to ride. Like a concert violinist who can feel, hear, and then tune his instrument, we become acquainted with our bodies.

Our breathing hastens and sweat begins to drip down our flushed faces; a global pain intensifies as we persist. Reaching the summit, we pedal the last few strokes with abated intensity knowing the effort is over. There is a mental and physical release and a rush of adrenaline. Above us the sky is a calming blue, while below us the villages, their houses looking like tiny ocher blemishes, spot the green and brown rural landscape of olive groves, woods, and farms. The view from the top is glorious.

We stop at the roadside, reach for our drinks, breathe slowly and deeply, and sip from the bottle.

The moment is one in a day of many similar moments that will leave me content in a way I have never felt in anything else. The sensation is unparalleled.

We are two cyclists on a climb, drained from an effort with several hours of riding to go; what we are doing is simplistic yet what we are experiencing is profound in the same way as yoga is cleansing for some, and church is a sanctuary for others.

Yet not all days are enriching. Waking up tired, lethargic, and with little motivation to pedal, training becomes mundane and the job a chore.

Descending the mountain our legs spin freely as we wind our way down the mountainside, cutting the corners, passing cars, and accelerating on the straightaways. Our tyres flick up scattered stones and our brakes squeal under the applied force. The tarmac is still wet in the late afternoon, as the December sun won't climb high enough in the sky to dry the road. We ride cautiously but well above an amateur cyclist's limit. Driving a car I would move down the mountain slower as it is a vehicle in which I fear the worst; on a bicycle I am cautious but rarely frightened.

On our bikes we loop around the countryside daily for two months. No ride is the same yet the objective remains the same: to progress.

Training alone or in pairs through November and December builds our fitness. However to race with a team and race well, we mentally and physically adapt again at our team training camps in January. In the autumn and winter months we have strengthened our muscles by lifting weights, working our core, and riding at a steady rhythm for prolonged periods. Our physique is strong and our health has rebounded after time away from the races, yet we are still unprepared to compete. The transition is significant.

Each of the dozens of professional squads will meet in late December or early January to ride together in a warm climate with quiet, undulating roads. When the cyclists arrive at the camp, they are a group of individuals on a roster. If the camp is well organised and if the riders spend four to seven hours a day for ten days together, they become a team. If the team is to win, the riders will need to make sacrifices for team and team-mates. Like firefighters going into a blaze or soldiers going into battle, we will need to develop a bond of trust and mutual respect. Each individual will find his confidence by knowing that each of his team-mates will drain himself of every watt of energy for the goal and will never relent until the job is done. Without a bond, a team can be successful but it will never find the consistency to become great.

In small groups, we arrive at the camp from around the world. Like the first day of school there is nervousness as we try to settle into the environment and find our niche. Our hotel rooms, which we share with a team-mate, are heaped with bags of new clothing. The aroma of plastic, fabric and ink is overwhelming. By dinner we will look like a team, as we will all be clothed identically in logoed tracksuits and t-shirts. Despite being in my 14th season as a professional, pulling on a new team jersey brings me a youthful sense of happiness and accomplishment.

At home in Girona, my day is loosely structured as my training times bend to my family's needs and appointments. At the team camps, our lives are scheduled to the minute, as the group is dependent on each individual. Nightly, we are handed schedules which outline the coming day's activities: breakfast, training length and workout specifics, lunch, massage, stretching and dinner. Slowly, our lives are being structured around the season and from January until autumn, cycling will virtually be our sole focus.

Ten months of the year will be spent on the new bikes that we ride for the first time at the training camp. Like putting on a new pair of shoes, there is a slow adaptation to a new bike. We each adjust the position so it suits our unique riding style or body type. No two riders will have the same position and we will spend days changing our saddle height, the saddle, the handlebars, or the frame size before we reach a point where the bike feels like ours.

The bike needs to become an extension of the body to the point where movements become innate. With time, the stiff saddle conforms to our unique anatomy. As the bike becomes wholly ours,we gain confidence in the way it handles and find the comfort that allows us to fly.

The camps are not only held to bring the riders together and to get them into condition for the season but also to finalise the logistics. We meet with the directeurs to determine which races we will ride and where our objectives will be – we will only reach a few peaks in fitness during the season and they will need to be timed to obtain the maximum reward.

Every day the team of 25 is divided into three separate groups. We will ride for three to six hours, punching our way up the climbs and spinning across the flat land in echelons. The training is programmed around future objectives. Training intensity and duration determine fitness,which is why the riders who will race imminently ride at higher intensities for longer periods than those who begin their racing season at the end of the month.

Like labourers tiring from a hard day at work, we stop for a coffee break when the rhythm lags late into the training session. When the moment is right and the café welcoming, the team comes to a halt and invades. Climbing off our bikes, unaccustomed to walking after pedalling for hours, we stretch momentarily before gathering around the bar to order drinks. In a flash of uniformity and colour, the café is briefly changed with our bikes piled against the wall outside and the directeurs' team cars parked in front. Our colourful outfits contrast with the drab blues and greys of the workmen who sit with us at the bar, but just like them we chat jovially before getting back to work under the setting sun.

It is on the bike that we become a team. The pouring rain, the blowing wind, and the hours in the saddle all converge to create a bond. When we return from our rides, there is a sense of achievement that only a cyclist who has ridden and suffered for hours in tough conditions knows and can relate to. After a hot shower, we warm up further over tea and cake. We chat like school-mates. The riders new to the team circle the clusters of team-mates, trying to enter or initiate conversations, while those who have been together for a few seasons converse with a jovial juvenile comfort.

On the bike, we learn more about each other than we will ever know in conversation. A rider's insecurities, weaknesses, and strengths are revealed in training and in races. Cycling somehow strips away the veil that we so often wear in social settings. Within days it is evident which riders will make sacrifices for the team and which will race selfishly for their own objectives.

Teams can function with a few individuals, especially if those individuals are able to win, but such teams will not work cohesively or win with any consistency. Often a good leader will work for his team-mates when he is not in a position to win, repaying them for work done. Each year, there are a few young riders who cannot accept the role of domestique and soon find themselves cast aside, isolated from the group, and eventually without work. When a neo pro arrives in a professional team, nothing he has done before is of any consequence – he must prove himself, and only with experience and strong performances will he gain the respect of his team-mates. In today's culture, young riders seem more consumed with the end result – the momentary glory and fame.

Whether a rider will make it is not only apparent on the bike but also at the dinner table. Christian Rumeau told me a story of a young neo pro who had golden palmarès as an amateur, including a World Championship medal. Christian had signed the rider to his team, RMO, which was at the top of French cycling during the early 1990s. But they knew before the season started that he would not develop into the champion many had predicted. The young pro arrived at the team training camp in southern France arrogant and self-assured. To his team-mates, who had won Tour stages, polka dot jerseys and Classics, his results were insignificant. Veteran team leaders, like RMO's Charly Mottet, value work ethic and respect over performances. After a long day of training, the team sat together at a long dining room table, munching on chunks of baguette and chatting as they waited patiently, starving, for their meal. When the plates of pasta arrived at the table the young pro put his hand out to take the first plate and dug in immediately. Mottet waited patiently for his plate and watched the youngster rudely munch away. With poor manners and disrespect for the leaders, the neo pro determined his fate within the team with one small gesture and his career as a professional only lasted a few years.

All professional cyclists are talented athletes but they must also be able to work and live with a team – a life not every person can adapt to. In cycling the margin of difference in physical ability between the best and worst is only a few per cent, magnifying the importance of the mind. A coach can improve performance but will struggle to change character, morals and values.

The physical tests the trainers and doctors run on our bodies at the training camp are done to determine the potency of our engines. Like mechanics looking under the hood of a car to run diagnostics, we are hooked up to machines, ride a stationary bicycle, and pedal until we collapse onto the handlebars, exhausted, but the tests are flawed if run to discover future champions. Like computer-generated art, the machine ignores human emotions: drive is often what separates a winner and a contender.

In 1996, when I was a young amateur racing in France, technological equipment was sparse in the peloton. We rode without two-way radios, the trainers didn't have access to mobile laboratory testing equipment and, although we occasionally rode with heart rate monitors, the powermeter was a rare piece of technology only used by a select few elite professionals. At our training camps, Christian Rumeau, our directeur, would sketch out a route based on what he thought we needed and then, while driving behind us, he would toot his horn when he wanted us to accelerate up a climb, or sprint towards a town. Christian would often call us back to the car to give us advice like a basketball coach might take his player aside to teach him how to hold the ball differently. Rumeau's eyes watched for every detail and missed few.

Lacking technology, he relied on his intuition, developed through a lifetime in cycling and, notably, during the 14 years that he directed teams to Classic and Grand Tour victories. When speaking with other managers and friends, he would talk about a rider's position, his potential and his style. His predictions were rarely off – all of his knowledge was built on experience.

Technology can be used to help train a cyclist but it cannot determine who will rise to the top. Conversely, it is often misguided. Had the T-Mobile management followed the coaches' advice to fire Mark Cavendish based on his poor test results, they would never have won more races than any other team in the peloton for two consecutive seasons. The fiercest fighters do not win because of their brawn but because of their desire.

By the end of the training camp we are ready to race – the team has goals to meet and expectations to fulfil. Paid to race we are expected to perform; we know our responsibility as individuals and as a team. And as individuals we carry the weight of responsibility to the team, as each of us determines the success of the whole.

In the few months of winter training we will have changed. Our bodies will have slimmed, our legs will be lean and our minds focused as our lives have become pointed and regimented. With thousands of kilometres, hundreds of specific workouts, and training in the gym, our physique will have slowly adapted.

Riding in a group at camp pains our leg muscles differently than the steady rhythm ridden at home. Together, we ride faster than we do alone, but work less as we spend more time sitting in the draft of team-mates. The change of speed is evident, as different pairs of riders increase or decrease the tempo as they take their turns at the front. The fluctuations are different from what my legs are accustomed to from riding alone and this noticeably affects my muscles. The change is another reason the camps are held; I can train properly alone but the required adaptation turns into progression in fitness.

After training together and pushing each other, we are virtually ready to race. There are many moments when training becomes a game – our innately competitive spirits inspire juvenile races. We challenge each other with the same fervour with which we will race shortly after the camp, simply because we love the game. The same spark we felt as kids racing around the city block is still evident as we sprint each other for town signs and hilltops.

The camp is the last time in the long season that the entire team will be together. We will return home for a short week or two before our bags are packed for the races. Although our homes are a base between the races, our suitcases will remain packed through the season, only emptied to be laundered and then repacked for the next event, as we are never home long enough to settle in.

After the short winter of training, our focus shifts to the imminent races. During the first decade of the new millennium, the racing season grew longer and more intense. The level of the peloton rose and the races became consistently more demanding from January until October. No longer do riders ease into the season, losing their Christmas fat during the races. Now we must be sharp, lean and fit from the first events. A decade ago the peloton splintered on climbs as the level of fitness was lower and the discrepancies greater whereas now the group rarely fractures and races arrive in massive sprints as the differences between riders and teams are slight. With each season the margins of victory decrease as the level of competition rises. No team wants to lose an inch on its rivals at any time even though there are 250 days to produce results.

During the training camp our mindset changes. We begin our winter training with a piece of wood which becomes a club at the first camp and by the end of January the club has become a spear. We work to keep that spear sharp for ten months and hope it never snaps or dulls – and by late October, at the Worlds, the commitment to the goal remains.

Lying on my back, with my feet hanging off the end of the small bed, I stare at the ceiling as my mind begins to fade in and out of sleep. Shafts of streetlight shine through the drawn shades and light up a few inches of the cream plaster above me. Deep in sleep, my team-mate turns in bed, flips over his pillow, and mumbles. A car speeds past the hotel, its tyres whirling on the wet pavement. Rain patters on the window. If the rain continues into the day, the race will be harder. But it will also be easier for me. In the cold and wet, the most tolerant and mentally resilient can persist. Dozens or more are eliminated – not through lack of physical strength but because they don't have the will.

In the shaft of light, I envision the roads I will ride, the winding course, the corners, the roundabouts and the descent – the smooth tarmac will be slick. I see a crash; I see myself crashing. I suppress the thought. Gliding through the corner, I accelerate as I travel out of it, attacking my pursuers. Behind, the peloton crumbles into ones and twos as riders fight to hold the wheel in front of them under the plumes of water, which spray from the wheels. Their legs are giving out beneath each push of the pedals. Five kilometres to go. Three more corners, a small climb and a straightaway are all that separates me from victory. I have spent 11 months training and preparing for the moment. And a lifetime. *La Flamme Rouge* is in sight. The red triangle, which hangs above the road to signal the last kilometre, blows at an angle. I am alone pedalling. Emotion overwhelms pain.

   I close my eyes to fall asleep. I am ready to race.

SRM Training System - (22/01/09 17.14 - 23.20 MiBa 5.48h 4258kj 170Km 11.8°c.)

Power [watt] —— Speed [km/h] —— Temperature [°]° Cadence [rpm] —— Heartrate [bpm] +

Altitude [m]   Training

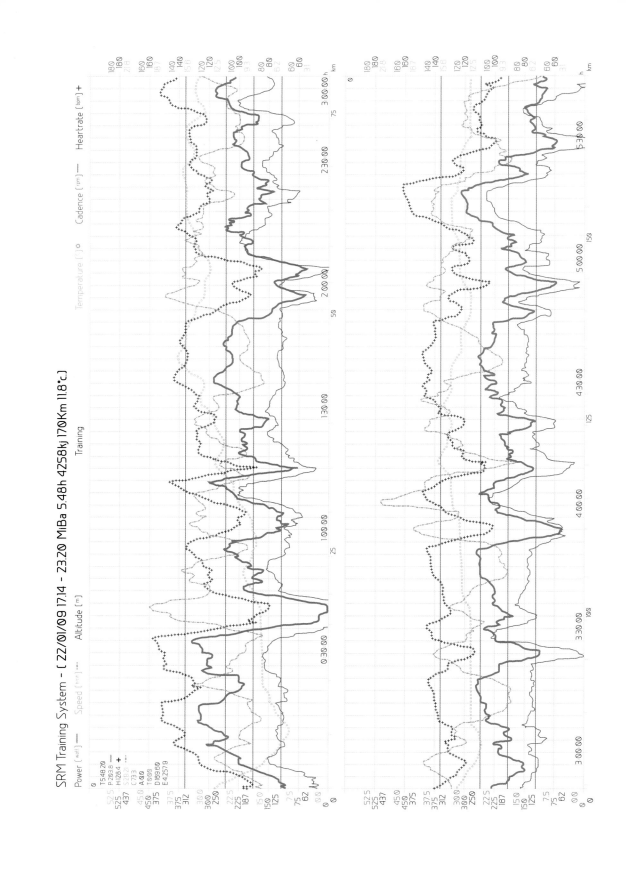

Girona, Catalonia, December 2008

RIGHT E-mail stop. Les Encies, Catalonia

LEFT Somewhere in Catalonia. December 2008

RIGHT: La Fageda, Olot, Catalonia. (Michael Rogers, Millar, Barry, Dan Martin)

LEFT: Cake stop. 50 kilometres from Girona

PREVIOUS PAGE: Palol de Revardit, Catalonia. December 2008

Gym Leader I. Girona. December 2008

LEFT: El Mallol, Catalonia I. December 2008

RIGHT: El Mallol, Catalonia II. December 2008

LEFT: Poblat Ibèric de la Palomera. (Millar and Barry). November 2009

RIGHT: Resting at the top of the Muntanya de Rocacorba climb

LEFT: Can Gubau, Anglès, Catalonia
(Millar, Barry, Martin)

RIGHT: Warming up with other tradesmen in a café,
Can Gubau, Anglès, Catalonia

OVERLEAF: Michael and David ride up the dirt road that leads
to Pantà de Susqueda, Catalonia

Modernist shelter, Pantà del Pasterel, Catalonia, December 2008

I sheltered for a while – shattered, freezing cold and wet. Michael, David and Dan battled on. It was a hard slog getting back to them. I was on a Vespa

OPPOSITE: Pantà de Susqueda, Catalonia

SPRING

I opened my eyes, confused. But the whirring and tapping that repeated with an irritating rhythm triggered a memory. I had no idea why I was in this machine, with my neck, legs and arms locked down and in place. The trapped feeling invoked panic. How long had I been in this chamber? Minutes, seconds, hours? Time passed and I was slowly, mechanically, rolled out of the tube and onto a bed. Flemish voices chattered over the noise of the machinery. Another memory. But still, I was unable to place where I was, and why I was here. I had been in MRI and CT scanners seemingly every year of my cycling career: the cream colour of the machine and the buzzing sounds in the clinical environment were all too familiar. But Flemish? Belgium?

The voices grew louder and then were above my motionless head. My eyes shifted up, down, then side to side to get a good look around at the room, at the two faces that stood on either side of me. One side came in clearer than the other which was troubling. Normally I could move freely in these machines, if I wanted to. Now, I couldn't. I was locked down.

With each movement of my face or my eyes, it burned in a familiar way: the burn caused by stone searing skin on impact. My body is covered in scars from a lifetime of injuries. With time the scars have become a part of me like tattoos on a rock star. Most of the cuts were never deep but they stung with a draft of air or touch of fabric; the familiarity of the burning on my face told me I had crashed.

With my eyes closed I saw a flash of the past. An image of a corner, a crowd, a barrier, paving stones. I was racing.

"How are you, Michael?" asked someone. Was he a doctor or a nurse?
"Where am I?"
"Roeselare. Do you know in what race you were riding?"
A race. I had likely crashed in a race and was in the hospital. I couldn't think of which. *Think*. Nothing. A mid-summer stage race came to mind.
"Region Wallonne?"
"No, the Ronde van Vlaanderen," the Flemish voice said. "You had an accident in Roeselare. Can you move your toes, your legs, for me?"
"My legs?" Oh, my God. I hate this fucking sport. "Can I see my son? Can you call my wife? I need to see my son now! I have a young son and I need to see him now!" Nothing else mattered. Tears that hadn't formed in a decade welled up in my eyes. "God, I don't care if I never ride again, I just want to see my son."
My toes moved. The man whose face I still really hadn't seen, and never would, patted me on the arm. "That's good. We will wait a few more minutes until the results of the scan of your spine are in."
The neck brace held me tight as the nurses began to clean my wounds. Tears streamed down my face and pooled up in the foam and metallic bit that held my neck still. Tears of fear of the unknown, tears for my family, and tears for my son. "Where are my son and my wife?"
This wasn't how the childhood games we played on our bikes had played out.

I imagined myself racing to victory in Flanders, across the fields where Merckx splintered pelotons and where our war heroes had battled and died.

"They are coming with your father. We just had a phone call from the team. They are on their way." The voice was somehow soothing – perhaps because she was just saying words I wanted to hear.

Time passed. Minutes, hours. It was all the same. I couldn't feel the pain of the wounds being cleaned of dirt and gravel. My mind was elsewhere, focused on my son. My pain was with him; my terror was that I would never see him again.

With my right eye I could clearly see the tiny television in the top right corner of the room, broadcasting images of cyclists that were clear enough for me to identify a rider by his position on his bike. After having ridden with them for tens of thousands of kilometres, their pedal stroke, the way they sat on their bikes, the way they accelerated were unique and individual, like an artist's brush stroke, and from any angle a trained eye could tell one cyclist from another in a peloton of 200 pedalling at 55 km/h.

Two hours before, I was pedalling in the peloton that I now watched on television. The race was the Tour of Flanders, the Ronde van Vlaanderen, the most important of the Belgian one day Classics, drawing hundreds of thousands of international spectators and the attention of the entire country.

The television in the room focused on the action in the race. I had arrived in the hospital room just in time to catch the finale out of the corner of my one good eye. The other was bandaged over and blown up like a boxer's after a knockout. The brace and spinal board no longer held my body down but I was to remain still in bed, on my back, as three vertebrae were fractured. The fractures weren't as bad as they'd thought, as they were only compression fractures: if the vertebra was a box, the top had been punched in from the impact.

My body was slowly being destroyed by bike crashes. Since I was a kid I had been breaking bones. A quick count put my broken bone total at 14: six vertebrae, femur, radial head, three ribs, nose, two wrists and a finger. Only two of those had not been broken while riding a bicycle.

Every rider in the peloton has scars and a story. Unafraid and without deep scars, young riders dive into corners while the veterans race more cautiously as the damage already done calms their fearless aggression. A bad crash drives sense into a rider – rarely does fearlessness make a champion.

During the early months of the year, from January until March, we race in week long stage races and one day road races to prepare for the Classics. These preparation races, while difficult to win, don't hold the same prestige as the one day races in late March, April and May. The bookies base their odds on riders' performances in the early races as they note their progression in fitness, their results, and their demeanour on the bike. Some champions float through the events with ease, testing their legs on occasion, but holding back to save their fitness for the Classics. Others prefer to attack in the preparation events and fight for the victory to gain confidence and needed fitness to tune their bodies and minds.

The Classics attract massive crowds and international television audiences because of the difficulty and because of their history. The group of riders on a team who will form the Classics squad will race and train together in the months prior to the events. To win they will need a bond built on trust, respect and experience.

We reconnoitre the courses to preview the technical sections, test equipment, and grow as a team. During those training sessions there is an excitement within the group. The Classics incite emotion even in the veteran mechanics, directeurs and riders, as we all know the stakes. Each of the staff has a vital role in preparing the cyclists for the battles we will encounter and they care for us as if they too were pedalling.

I had a stake in the Ronde. I was *en forme*, two of my team-mates were the favourites and my family had flown from North America to cheer at the roadside. Lying in a hospital and unsure if I would ever be able to race again, my life came into perspective as I had left the insular world of professional cycling the moment I crashed. Only a few hours before the accident, we were all in the bus, plugging in our two-way radios and placing them in the backs of our shorts, packing food in our pockets and nervously fidgeting with wrappers, plastic coffee cups, stir sticks or helmet straps as we waited for the call to the start line. The Tour of Flanders was the first of the big three for the Classics team. It is arguably the toughest week in the sport, beginning with the Tour of Flanders, a 250 kilometre race over tiny cobbled farm roads on an undulating and sinuous course, and ending with Paris-Roubaix, a 270 kilometre race over the roughest cobbled roads in France. Sandwiched in between the two is a lesser Classic, Gent-Wevelgem. It is a race that is won in the crosswinds, which blow with force off the North Sea and frequently shatter the peloton within the first kilometres of the 200 kilometre race.

Cobbles are uncomfortable to drive over when sitting in a Mercedes. But on a bike, you feel every one of the granite stones as the wheels bounce and bang over them; the resounding vibration that rattles every piece of the skeleton from toes to fingertips. My first time over the cobbles, I woke up the next morning thinking the flu had set into my bones, but my room-mate corrected me, saying: "It is the stones that make the body ache that badly."

Despite the injuries I return to the northern European roads every year. The sensation of completing a Classic, or riding on the front of the peloton over the cobbles, is unlike any other I have lived. Television images of the peloton in a single line floating over the cobbles come close to capturing the beauty of the event, what we feel and why we race.

My grandfather, a western Canadian who grew up on an isolated ranch near Medicine Hat, Alberta, told me to stop riding when I was ten years old as he thought the pain was abnormally damaging. When I didn't relent, he scolded my mother for allowing me to ride so hard, pushing my body to its limit. The expression of pain on my face was telling, which made him believe racing was unhealthy. Grandpa had lived through the drought and depression of the 1930s, survived the bleakest coldest winters on the open prairie, fractured dozens of bones while breaking horses, and knew suffering beyond what I could ever imagine, but his world was far from mine, which made it impossible for him to understand bike racing.

My mother, who became a cyclist after meeting my father, slowly developed an understanding of the sport as she quickly realised it was the only way they would be able to spend time together. She understood the passion. Twenty five years later she still prays nightly as she knows the dangers I face every day, yet also realises the importance the bike has in my life so she asks God that I meet my goals. She never questions my goal and my career, but I know she prays.

The massive granite cobblestones are not what scare me. On them I feel oddly in control. It is the panic they cause as the peloton races towards the cobbled sectors – this is what makes them frightening. Riders racing in fear cause the worst crashes. They tense and, with arms gripping the handlebars, are more apt to make erratic moves; one mistake creates a domino effect, sending racers crashing down.

In the flatter one day races, the Tour of Flanders, Gent-Wevelgem, Milan-San Remo, and Paris-Roubaix, the peloton races with a unique intensity. The riders have each made sacrifices for months to prepare for the events. Each rider has trained, dieted, slept and, for some, doped, in his own meticulous way, and most have been aspiring to perform in these races since they were children.

A performance, whether it is a victory or simply a potent attack at the right moment, can change a rider's career. A victory will ensure his place in the history books, an increase in salary, bonuses and fame. A well timed attack will show he has potential, panache and desire. Each rider who has prepared for the race wants to separate himself from the rest, but most will only just survive while dozens will not even make it to the finish line. In every race there is a chance that something may go wrong: a mechanical failure, a crash or a flat tyre. But in the Classics the stakes are higher, the risks greater, and the odds of puncturing or crashing at the wrong moment utmost. Everything can be lost in a moment, a second, or less. Our devotion to the bikes creates an all-or-nothing mentality on the day of the race. Everything in our lives seems to come down to one day of racing and perhaps even just one moment in the day.

Cycling has traditionally been a working class sport. From the first races over a century ago, a bicycle became an escape from the mines, the fields and the factories. Young men saw the opportunity to evade a predestined future by racing a bike. With nothing to lose and idolatry, wealth and prestige to gain, they devoted themselves to their new job. Cycling is not only a sport or pastime but also a lucrative profession compared to a bricklayer's life.

Cyclists, especially those from northern Europe, are hardened and tough. The environment, the races and the culture change a person. Only the mentally and physically strong survive; the toughest of the Classics riders were raised

LIVRET DE SANTE

Nom : ....BARRY..........

Prénom : ....MICHAEL..........

Nationalité : ....CAN..........

No de licence : ....47031..........

Licence délivrée par : CANADIAN CYCLING A.

Code UCI : CAN 19751213

Adresse : PUJADA St. DOMENEC 3

Code Postal et Ville : 17004 GIRONA

Pays : SPAIN

Signature du coureur : ....

Equipe : TEAM COLUMBIA / HIGHROAD

Nom du Médecin responsable de l'Equipe et Signature :

0486/09

with a fighter and survivor mentality. The Dutch world champion Hennie Kuiper said: "It is a sport where you eat the other rider's lunch first." Some cyclists will do whatever necessary to survive, to win, or to profit.

At any of the start lines in Belgium or northern France, the duress of the lives lived can be seen on the spectators' faces. Bundled in layers of grey, navy and forest green clothing to protect themselves from the elements, the crowd is proletarian in appearance – not consumed with vanity but full of hardened humility, they wave their yellow Flandrian flags, chant songs to encourage their favourites, and drink Belgian beer at 10am as if it were late in a night of festivities. Their cheers are rooted in both passion and a sense of profit as the spectators encourage their favourites not only because they are fervent fans but also because many have bets placed with the local bookies. To them, the Tour de France, the Giro d'Italia, or the countless other races of prestige during our season are secondary to the cobbled Classics. The races somehow provide a break in the dreary damp spring, a festival to celebrate the bike. The races, which have criss-crossed the rural landscape for over a century, were only interrupted by the two World Wars when the farm fields became battlefields. In Belgium, bike racing has the social status of dog racing elsewhere: the races are bet on, the cyclists are driven until they fail, and the drunken crowds spit beer at their fallen heroes.

During his cycling career, while living and racing in Belgium, the Dane Brian Holm would only read novels relating to the two Great Wars. Although the Danes are known for their tenacity in adverse conditions, even he found the conditions in Belgium challenging. Daily, Holm raced and trained through the fields that the soldiers had fought and died on. The riding was tedious as the wind blew the thrashing rain sideways, the mud and manure dragged onto the roads by the tractors flicked into his face, and the chill in his bones never seemed to leave until the summer sun shone. For years, to strengthen his constitution and bring perspective, he read novel after novel of the terrors the young boys had endured in the trenches in Flanders fields. Somehow, it gave him purpose, motivated him, and made his job easier.

The environment is hauntingly grim in the winter and spring. The mist lies low below the grey skies and the countryside is damp, brown, and green. Racing through it, there is an eerie sense of the past, or perhaps it is my knowledge of the horrors and what those boys endured that haunts. The races take us through towns and fields familiar from high school textbooks and grandparents' stories yet neither were able to clearly convey the bleak environment. It wasn't until I had felt the dampness, the grey skies and slashing rain, and had ridden through these fields that I had any real concept of the terror of the battles. We are only bike racers yet we often struggle to endure the races – perspective makes our weakness seem pathetic.

In the race bag, there is everything that might protect me in adverse conditions. Cyclists are at war with the weather. In the spring we freeze; in the summer we dehydrate. With a tailwind, the attacks never relent as the wind gives everybody in the peloton the false sense that he has the legs of a champion. A headwind saps our energy and we look for cover behind a wheel and a bigger body. With a strong wind, only the brave, strong or naive attack alone. The weather, like the courses, is never the same – the changing conditions create a dynamic race, which the cyclist either embraces or battles.

In the spring we have cold weather clothing, which we can only hope will keep us warm. Each rider finds combinations of clothing that work well for his body and somehow we place false confidence in the clothing, thinking it will protect us. It never does. We all freeze in cold rain. We are fortunate when we can make it through the first kilometres of a wet race without feeling the cold water slowly soak through the layers, down the ankles and into the shoes. Frozen fingers disable a cyclist: unable to shift his gears, pull the food out of his pockets, or squeeze his water bottle, dreams of victory are replaced by hopes of simply surviving.

In the cold, the mentally tough, conditioned and aware, race while the others, defeated when they wake in the morning to rain on the window, simply pedal because they must. The riders fight for the victory at the front of the peloton while those behind fight to make it to the finish. Daily, every rider has his goal and battle and whether it is internal or external, the goal and the struggle evolve through the season. We all seek the moment where suffering can be pushed from our thoughts as it is overwhelmed by the emotion of fluidity on a bike.

In the Classics, and in flatter races, a power-to-weight ratio is not significant in predicting performance. The bulk of muscle needed to propel a bike forward does not need to be carried uphill. But when mountains and hills loom, the ratio between power and weight becomes a decisive factor. Climbers, like distance runners, become near-anorexics to reach the ideal power-to-weight ratio of close to seven watts per kilo while the Classics men race at a heavier weight than they will in the Tour de France or Giro d'Italia. On the cobbles, like in the wind, brute force moves the bicycle quickest.

When a rider is *en forme*, he can fly through the spring as most cyclists can maintain a peak in fitness for roughly a month. Packed into a week, with good luck, he can perform consistently and achieve his targets.

George Hincapie, my good friend and team-mate, has ridden with that one week in mind with devotion and unwavering focus through each winter and spring for the past 16 years before turning his focus to his domestique's duties in the Tour de France. As a boy growing up in Queens, New York, his bulky frame won him sprints, criteriums and the flatter road races. George's mind has been focused on Paris-Roubaix – on the legendary velodrome, the cobbles and the crowds – since he raced around Central Park before dawn as a young schoolboy. Despite his focus and meticulous preparation, he has yet to win the Tour of Flanders or Paris-Roubaix. His career has been one of almosts as he has been on the podium, won the less prestigious Gent-Wevelgem, and consistently been among the protagonists.

Hincapie sits low on the bike, his legs turning a smooth cadence. Between the Classics and the Tour de France he will lose three to four kilograms as his job and focus change. A rider who has spent most of his life on his bike, he seems more comfortable on it than off: in town he walks slowly, ambling through the streets in Girona, and in a chair he slouches as his back is curved from sitting in the saddle and his shoulders crunched from holding the handlebars. His body seems uncomfortable and unaccustomed to movement off the bicycle but posed on a bike his lean, scarred and muscular body exudes power. Prior to the Classics, he rides with vision. He knows how to train properly, yet there is still a childlike excitement in him in the weeks prior to the races.

The one season in his long career that he missed the Classics because of illness, George fell into depression. Stuck at home, unable to ride, he felt lost and without purpose. For most of his life he had either ridden in the spring while dreaming of riding the Classics or had been preparing himself to win. Cyclists become singularly focused and without the focus there is a void which can only be filled by riding. On the bike we find a high, and it becomes an obsession. The sensation is laced with a buzz of endorphins, a rhythmic directed life, and an elation from accomplishment whether it is from a training ride, summiting a mountain, or reaching the finish line.

As a domestique, most of my career has been spent at the service of my team-mates. George is not only a friend but also a rider whom I protect from the wind, keep fuelled with drinks and food, and position for the decisive moments of the race. Our relationship on the bike has developed to a point where decisions are made without words being spoken; there is a mutual confidence between the two of us. His victory is also mine.

A rider who knows the tiny rural roads well, who trains on them often and who has raced on them since his youth, has a greater chance of winning a Classic. In over a century of racing, the Belgians and northern Europeans have dominated the results while the Italians have earned sporadic victories by specialists who have focused their careers on the races.

In a career spanning 16 years, Gilbert Duclos-Lassalle, a Frenchman with a passion for Paris-Roubaix, won the race twice near the end of his career. His victories came with experience. Like a master chef who cooks without recipes but with savoir-faire, the rider needs knowledge, instinct, power and panache to win a Classic. Races can be formulaic in structure but the Classics are so intensely contested, and so physically difficult, that a command of the minutiae can mean the difference between being a contender and being a winner.

As he reaches the last years of his career, Hincapie may finally have the knowledge to win. A foreigner, he hasn't had the advantages of the northerners who have known the roads and the way the peloton will race since adolescence. While he was in Central Park, they were already on the cobbles. Sixteen years into his career, Hincapie now knows the roads better than most.

But perhaps he is too gentle to win. Rivals have told me repeatedly that George was too friendly, too calculating, and didn't take enough risks to win.

There are maybe a dozen opportunities to win in a race, sometimes fewer, but if a rider doesn't attack and gamble, he won't win. A cyclist can calculate – using his experience to figure out the race tactics in the finale – but to win a Classic he must rely on instinct. Like a torero fighting a bull, a rider can wear down the competition with repeated bursts, but only one attack – the final sword deciding how the bull dies – determines whether he will win or lose. In a race that follows a pattern, it is in the finale that the rider must use his savoir-faire to forge the winning advantage. His timing must be precise. One wrong move, and his energy is depleted and his chances of winning are diminished. George has learned to calculate and divide the race into sections from having ridden for Lance Armstrong, yet his results on paper haven't equalled his qualities as an athlete. Arguably he would have won far more races on another team, and perhaps he would have learned how to properly execute the final attack as he would have had more opportunities to lead the team. At the Tour de France, his role within the team was that of selfless domestique who prepared the terrain for his leader, Armstrong, and therefore he was rarely in a position to deal the final blow.

To win the rider needs to take a chance, yet confidence determines the outcome. A rider who believes the moment he attacks is the right one, believes he has the legs to go all the way to the finish, and believes his team is there to support him will win. The bike floats beneath the confident rider. He looks back only to see how large the gap that he has opened is and then pushes on towards the finish line. As soon as a rider looks back again and questions his ability to win, the odds are much greater that he will be caught and fail. A look over the shoulder shows his weakness, that his mind is questioning his legs' ability to push the pedals, and that his focus is taken away from the objective of winning the race while he gives in to the fear of being caught.

The Classics strip cycling to the bone, which is what attracts millions of spectators and invokes such emotion in the crowds. The athlete and the machine are pushed to their limits in a six hour crusade of suffering, danger, triumph and defeat. There is a photograph of Hincapie taken after the 2002 Paris-Roubaix that captures the race, the Classics, and true cycling. He is sitting on a filthy concrete shower bench in the velodrome in Roubaix. His body is covered in mud, the sponsors' logos on his clothing are indecipherable, and his credit card sized race radio lies discarded on the floor. His low slung head is held between his hands: he is completely defeated, shattered mentally and physically by the weather, the race, his adversaries and himself. He told me that the photo is what motivates him to go back to Roubaix each season.

As leader of the team he failed in the final kilometres. After spending a long day in the wet and cold without consuming enough food, his body was no longer able to function properly and his brain became dull from lack of sugar. His muscles gave out and his bike lost the momentum that had made his effort look easy. Skidding, slipping, and finally crashing, he fell into a muddy ditch of deep rain water. George later told me that at that moment he wanted to curl up and go to sleep. But he couldn't. He climbed out, climbed on, and raced towards the finish. The performance of his team-mate, Tom Boonen, transcended any of his past results as the young Belgian neo pro placed a remarkable third. The moment was bittersweet. The Lion of Flanders, Johan Museeuw, had won his third Paris-Roubaix. On the podium, he told Boonen: "You are the next Johan Museeuw."

Cycling is pure and primitive as men are seen suffering at their utmost on a simple machine. In La Course en Tête, the film biography of Eddy Merckx, a journalist asks Eddy if he thinks cycling is popular because, quoting scientist and Nobel Prize winner Jacques Monod, "people admire courage, calculation and willpower, all of which are primitive instincts." Eddy quietly ponders the question and then nods his head in agreement.

Through the spring, while training in Girona, it is on the Catalan roads that Hincapie prepares his body and mind for the races. He can train consistently in a warmer climate, logging kilometres on the roads when others freeze in the cold northern European climate. He has chosen to exchange the cobbled roads for warmer weather. In Girona, the rides finish with a sprint in the old town, up a slippery cobbled Roman road – the closest thing to a Belgian berg in northern Spain.

The night before the race, all seems possible. After spending the spring together, racing throughout Europe and training at home, we sit together in a small yet elegant hotel room in the French countryside, watching a movie on a laptop. We are less than 12 hours from the start of Paris-Roubaix. As we watch the small screen that sits on a chair in between our cot-like beds, George massages his legs by shaking, digging, and kneading his trunk-like quads as a baker works a batch of dough. It is a habit all cyclists seem to pick up. Good legs or bad legs, a massage is always soothing and cyclists touch their legs like writers twirl their pens or pianists tap their fingers. Our legs are the instruments we need to perform.

On the back of the chair hang our jerseys, with the numbers pinned on the pockets, ready to go. There is an air of nervousness in the room that is veiled by the voices on the screen; the intensity of the show hides what is really going on in our minds. Too much is out of our control and the answers we are looking for can't be found in our legs or any sensation we have at that moment. The answers are on the road and in cycling, when emotions are wrapped into the odds, it is hard to bet on what will happen. In each of the eight seasons we have ridden together, he was a favourite, and each season it seemed this would be his year. Underdogs can't lose eternally and somewhere, eventually, he holds hope he will find what has so far been elusive in the 270 kilometres between the start and finish line.

Race days are broken down: transfer times, start time, time gaps, pedal strokes, feed zones, sprints, climbs, meals, meeting times, massage times, and a finish line. When I close my eyes to sleep, it all becomes a blur, the schedule is just a formality, and my stomach gets tight with thoughts of the race, the suffering, the tactics and the finish line. Images of the finish line push us beyond our fears.

The fear I drive from my mind before Paris-Roubaix is that of a crash. In a career of tumbles and slides, one crash has marked me mentally and physically. When I close my eyes I recollect images of the crash, which have re-entered my consciousness with time. I see the barrier, the corner, the paving stones, and the rider in front of me. In the final image, just before the sequence becomes black, I sense the feeling of disaster – the emptiness of being unable to control my life before it spins away. The scars have faded but the memory haunts me when I close my eyes the night before we race in Flanders or northern France. Suppressing the images I know they will soon fade. They always do.

In the bus, on the way to the start, there is a nervousness not felt at other events. Conversation is inane and unfocused, as the race weighs heavy on our thoughts. Some riders block out the chatter with music that blows through their massive headphones as they lean back with their heads firmly on the headrest. The music is played to isolate and relax them in their own world, away from distractions in the bus, while images of the race they must tackle flash behind their closed eyes. With a team and a leader that can win, the uncontrollable is what creates anxiety.

If someone speaks of crashes, everybody turns away. We sink our heads to avoid the topic, pretending to be preoccupied. Those who understand cyclists know that we don't speak of what scares us in the fear that it may happen. By avoiding the subject, by not listening to our fears, we somehow think we are protected. If we did calculate the risks and odds, we wouldn't race. In Paris-Roubaix, we prepare for the race and pray for protection.

Before the start, the team of riders prepares in the bus. Some tape their wrists for support while others nervously cut at fabric on their clothing and in their gloves to decrease friction. Everyone tries to find a way to make what he is about to endure less painful. Some carry ibuprofen, others aspirin, caffeine, or any other supplement or pill that will ease the pain, provide a mental and physical boost, and not show up positive on the drug tests. Some riders pulverise the pills into a powder, mix the powder with liquid sugar, and place it in a small flask, a bidon, in their back pocket. Others wrap up the pills in little foil packets, put them in their back pocket, or place them under the elastic band at the bottom of the lycra shorts. In a moment of duress, or just before the finale, they will dig in their pockets for the pills as they look for a boost.

As one rider loads his pockets with food, another empties his bowels one last time in the bus's cramped toilet, while another tests his radio and yet another has lotion applied to his legs by the soigneur. Preparation becomes a ritual. In the hour before the race, there is chaos in the bus as each rider readies himself in a routine he has developed in the countless races ridden since his youth. The soigneur methodically prepares each rider's legs for a quick rub down by rolling up the shorts and down the socks, so the leg muscles can be massaged with fluidity while also keeping the clothing clean. The coloured oil is applied for vanity as much as it is warmth; not only will the capsicum give the muscles a warming sensation but the red tint and thick oil will give them visual tone. The soigneurs' strokes are unique to each individual: limp hands do a perfunctory job while those with fluid and strong rhythm work with concern.

The peloton lines up under the start banner in a cobbled square in Compiègne, a small Parisian suburb. Riders continue their nervous chatter, check their tyre pressure one last time, compare bikes with their rivals as each has a special set-up they hope will endure the race, and munch on little bits of food to pass the long few minutes until we start. I gaze down at my front wheel, my arms resting on my handlebars and my head hung low. My body is relaxed while my mind is anxious to begin. Beyond my wheel are massive cobbles. Individually their tops are as smooth as tile but together the gaps between them cause the body to shudder – from experience I know there is a point where the cobbles will go from feeling like a road to a thousand little blows. I can only pray that moment comes late in the race. With good legs the road is a collage of stones that the bike glides over but when the body begins to fail, the stones jar as momentum is lost and focus becomes blurred.

When fears of rain for the race fade, our focus shifts to the wind. Strong persistent winds usually mean dry roads but tense racing from the start; the peloton races nervously as there is a fear of fractures in the group. The wind dries out the cobbles, making the racing faster, more dangerous and the chances of punctures greater. The bikes, cars and wind kick up clouds of dust that form over the racing peloton. We absorb the dust. Spitting it out and coughing it up, we choke on the clouds as the grimness builds with the distance. Hincapie, like most of the specialists, prefers the wet as skills become crucial, making the race selective and thinning the peloton so that only the experienced favourites are left at the front. Bike handling and experience become more important than luck. In the wet, outsiders are eliminated early but regardless of the weather, we always return to the goal: victory.

Inevitably, riders crash from nervousness in the first kilometres of the race. The peloton is jittery even though we have three hours until we reach the first sectors of pavé. A touch of wheels brings down a pile of riders and brakes squeal like pigs going to slaughter. Carbon snaps, riders yell, and the peloton flies away.

With a headwind the race is more dangerous as the peloton balloons; on the smooth roads the teams race for the front to place their leader in position for the cobbled sections, only to be reabsorbed by the peloton quickly as they can't hold the speed in the front against the wind. As they are reabsorbed, there is a continued fight for the front. Riders bump against each other in a panic: everybody wants to be in the front for the cobbles as they know it is the safest spot to be, and their directeurs are yelling through the radios that they need to move up in the peloton. There are only a few moments to relax and they come in the first metres of smooth roads after the cobbles. We sit up, drink, eat, and then refocus for the fight to the next section.

Whatever the weather – wet, dry, tailwind, crosswind, or headwind, the race is wildly chaotic and dangerous.

Teams will eat through their domestiques as the race progresses. In the first hours before the break is established, the peloton settles into a steady chase; three riders are responsible for following attacks and attacking as they try to place a rider in the break. The leaders will never follow the attacks as it is a waste of energy that will be needed in the finale. There is a tactical formula to a one day race. The strongest teams will position themselves within the structure of the race so that their leaders approach the finish as fresh, and as close to the front of the race, as possible. The winning attacks occur in the last hour of racing, while anything before is usually fruitless – the only purpose of those attacks being to pressure rival teams into chasing or to gain television exposure for the sponsors.

As the first cobbled sectors approach in Troisvilles, a small town known for its racing pigeons and place on the race course, the tension builds in the peloton. Domestiques stop with leaders to urinate at the road side as they know this may be the last opportunity. Excess clothing is stripped as we know our bodies are soon to heat up with the increased intensity. We drop back to the team cars for water bottles and food. Like a farmer preparing his farm for a coming storm, we ready ourselves in haste, knowing this is the final moment before the suffering begins.

We take notice of the landmarks that signal the poignant moments of the race. The water tower at the entrance to the horrendous Arenberg forest can be seen from kilometres away – the moment it is in sight, there is a surge as the peloton anticipates the pavé. The long road of rough cobbles that cuts through the dark forest will select the contenders from the group. Those who aren't with the leaders as they exit the forest stand little chance of winning.

As the race nears its end, the cobbled sectors come up quickly. The smooth bits of road linking the cobbled sections provide moments of relief. We grasp for bottles of water from the soigneurs who stand at the end of the sectors where the cobbles turn to smooth tarmac. The abrupt transition is significant. With fewer spectators on the tarmac, noise dissipates. The peloton, which rides in single file over the stones as each rider follows the less treacherous route, balloons again on the tarmac where riders can finally exchange a few words and refocus before the next sector. The pavement feels as smooth as tile. We readjust our bodies on the bike in the empty hope that somehow the next sector might be easier, even though we know they only get harder with the passing kilometres.

Each cyclist is ripping his muscles, draining his body, and sapping the sugar needed for his brain to function properly. Some have torn shorts, cut knees, swollen elbows, broken helmets and damaged bikes. All have scars they have accumulated since their first races as boys, which they will wear the rest of their lives. Yet we all pedal with a fury that only comes when there is a finish line and an end. For some the goal is to win, while for others it is simply to survive the race. Resigned and defeated riders persist for their pride as even finishing is unique and something for which they will be congratulated. Completing the race is a victory because that, in and of itself, is an extraordinary triumph.

The last sectors of cobbles, which are no more than three kilometres in length, seem endless in the last hour of the race. The spectators, many of whom have been at the roadside since the early morning to stake out their spot, are heavily inebriated after a day of drinking. Only at the last minute do they move off the road and out of the riders' path with a stumble and yell. As we enter the hordes lining the cobbled sectors, the smell of booze is vile in the way that a bar reeks of skanky beer the morning after a busy night. Beer is spilled on the cobbles and doused on riders. The fans, who are only centimetres from the riders, drunkenly exhort us as we speed through. Our single hope is that they won't step out and bring us to the ground. The day has been long and furious for everybody.

To endure the distance we set targets within the body of the race. Sectors, towns, kilometre markers and feed zones divide the race by breaking it down into manageable sections. In the hillier races, we gauge our day on the summits crested. Regardless of which race we are riding, everything is possible with 20 kilometres to go: roughly half an hour of racing is left. I can suffer in pain for half an hour, the breakaway can be caught, and the victory is possible. Seeing the sign I feel a change; the thought of the finish overwhelms everything else. My mind absorbs the pain and I pedal with adrenaline. Our lives have been built around this finale.

As my wheels touch the concrete velodrome in Roubaix, I am lifted into another space. I enter my childhood dream. I reach the sublime. The crowds are a blur, my legs painless, my body tingling, and my mind floating.

The moment passes once we lap around the track twice, and ride down the banking and out of the velodrome. The race is over and seven hours on the bike become but a few snapshots in my memory. The rest of the race melds together and fades. The moments I remember are those that drive me to return.

As we roll to the bus, the mechanics grab our bikes in haste, hose them down, and pack them up. Slowly, I step on to the bus. Team-mates hug one another. In contrast to the staff who hurriedly pack up the gear, the riders move slowly. The grey concrete velodrome showers resemble those in penitentiaries: the floor is cold and dirty, the air is damp, and the concrete is grim. Yet we linger under the shower, enjoying the hot water as it pours over our worn muscles. After six hours of panic and chaos, the moment seems idyllic. Food tastes better, chairs seem more comfortable, and being completely exhausted is divine.

My mobile phone blinks with messages from family, friends and fans transmitted as they've watched the race on television. The phone buzzes. It is a call from Christian Rumeau who calls me after every major event. He tells me that I looked good on the cobbles, that my position on the bike is as it should be, and then he reminds me of my errors. I listen. I learn. Rumeau has slowly become the little voice in the back of my head that always reminds me about *'le métier'*. How I must remain focused and devoted. I picture him on the other end of the line, in his small apartment in Annemasse, France, on his couch, in front of the television. "Eh, le Canadien! Félicitations." A compliment from Rumeau is worth more than a trophy and a kiss from the beauty queen.

Several days after the finish, my body is still sore. My hands are blistered, my wrists are swollen, and my joints ache. My leg muscles, damaged from crashing and from the effort, ache while my eyes expel sticky bits of grit. Many of the protagonists will take a few weeks to recover from their efforts on the cobbles while the domestiques will move on to the next races, the Ardennes Classics or the short week long spring stage races that will prepare them for the Giro d'Italia and Tour de France. For the rest of the team, there is no time to celebrate or rest as they move directly on to another race.

While training alone at home, my thoughts always move to the Classics. In those thoughts I find inspiration as I did as a teenager on the wintery streets of Toronto as I imagined I was racing in France. The thoughts drove me to ride for hours in the cold and dark. The same imagined scenarios still invoke desire to pursue the extreme. The difficulty of those races pushes me to exhaustion where I can find unparalleled fulfilment. It is an emotion few people will ever experience.

I saw the finale of the Ronde from my hospital bed. George stood on the third step of the podium. He'd had the legs to win, and his disappointment was apparent. In a Classic, where the stakes are highest, self-focused team-mates sometimes become rivals. Victories are bought and sold.

The phone rang.

"Michael. How are you? Sorry. Sorry. Fuck…" The voice of the team's press officer trailed off. He'd seen me lying on the road. The crash had appeared lethal.

"I am okay. Beat up, but I will be okay. I don't have a clue what happened. Did any of the guys see me crash?"

There had been blood pouring out of my face. It pooled on the tarmac around my head, while I was curled up and motionless as the riders, caravan and spectators all gazed and then sped on.

The sticky matted mess of dried blood and sweat on my face and in my hair disgusted me as I pressed the phone against my ear. Someone had said they would be around in a minute to clean the road dust and dirt off my legs, wipe down my body, and wash my hair. A shower wasn't an option, as I wasn't allowed to move from the bed or even twist and turn. For now I was stuck on my back until the surgeon reviewed the CT scan.

"George is here. He just got off the podium. He wants to speak with you. We'll come by the hospital as soon as we can."

There was a harsh reality to waking up alone in a foreign hospital and not having a clue what had happened, where I was, or what was going to happen.

I knew from past experience that racing transcends health. Cyclists are put back on their bikes with fractured bones. We race sick. We race coughing blood. The race is always the priority. But the team doctor should have been with me. It sickened me when I later heard – after one of my team-mates also crashed and went to another hospital – that he had lied to the rider's wife, saying he was at the hospital taking care of me, so he could stay at the race to be there for the glory at the finish.

"How are you?" George was on the phone. "I wanted to quit the race to go to the hospital with you but Dirk [our directeur] swore you were okay and that he had spoken to you. I was so scared when I saw you on the ground." His voice was monotone, morose and stressed.

"I am okay. Congrats on a great race. I don't think I ever spoke to Dirk. I don't recall a thing. I woke up in the hospital an hour after the crash." I felt ill.

The picked over, barely eaten hospital food that lay flatly on the plastic tray started to make my stomach turn. I regurgitated a chocolate. To lift my spirits, my wife Dede and my father had bought a box of chocolates that I opted to eat as dinner instead of the pale, tasteless hospital food.

They sat beside me quietly as I told them I wasn't sure I wanted to race any more, that I didn't know if it was worth the risk, and that I couldn't now that I was a father. Liam was asleep against Dede's breast. As I spoke I looked to my father for a reaction. I knew Dede would agree with whatever I was feeling as she had just retired from a career as a cyclist. She retired because she was tired of living in hotels and was scared of crashing heavily. With each race that fear increased.

"I don't care if I ever race again." My dad looked over and seemed to agree. This had perhaps been a longer day for him than for me. I was in a race he had read about every year since he was a teenager. He saw me attack early in the race, and then, when he and Dede expected me to pass them again, I wasn't in the group. A pit of fear formed in their stomachs. It was then, moments after the peloton had sped by, that the mobile phone rang and they were told to rush to the hospital.

Twenty five years after pedalling to victory in my first race in downtown Toronto, I was sitting in a hospital bed, contemplating the future and detesting the sport to which I had devoted my life.

Most cyclists complain incessantly about the difficulties. The sport kills the athlete's morale repeatedly as we suffer day after day. But this pain also leads to the incredible joy and sense of accomplishment when he crosses the finish line, triumphs in victory, or simply reaches the doorstep after a long day of training. In no other sport does an athlete feel defeat as often. The most successful professional cyclist in the world might win 20 of 100 races he enters, and most professionals go seasons, even careers, without a victory. We each have our own goals, our own finish lines. There is joy in the struggle and that struggle becomes an addiction rooted in the elation.

On the hospital bed I hated the sport, but somewhere I knew that I would pedal in a race again, that the passion was still down below the wounds of the crash. That passion would drive me. It had since my first crash and my first defeat.

And then, when George walked in the room, it became clear I had to race again.

His face was empty and gaunt from the efforts of the race, as he had spent six hours on his bike. He smiled when he walked into the room but quickly the smile vanished when he saw my face. To me, he looked drained and weak from the stress of the Ronde.

Now that George was in the room, and we were talking about the race, the coming races and the team, I wanted to be on my bike: riding, training, racing. 'Cyclist' was my identity. I could walk, so I could ride again. My thoughts flipped back and forth from loathing to loving, from quitting to pursuing. This was the cyclist's life: one of highs and lows, pain and jubilation, victories and defeats.

As he walked out the door, we wished each other well.

"You'll kill them all in Roubaix." I had a pit in my stomach as I thought about the coming races. I would miss the action on the road with the team, but as I looked over at Liam, sitting there on Dede's lap, I knew I could no longer take those risks.

But I also knew I would.

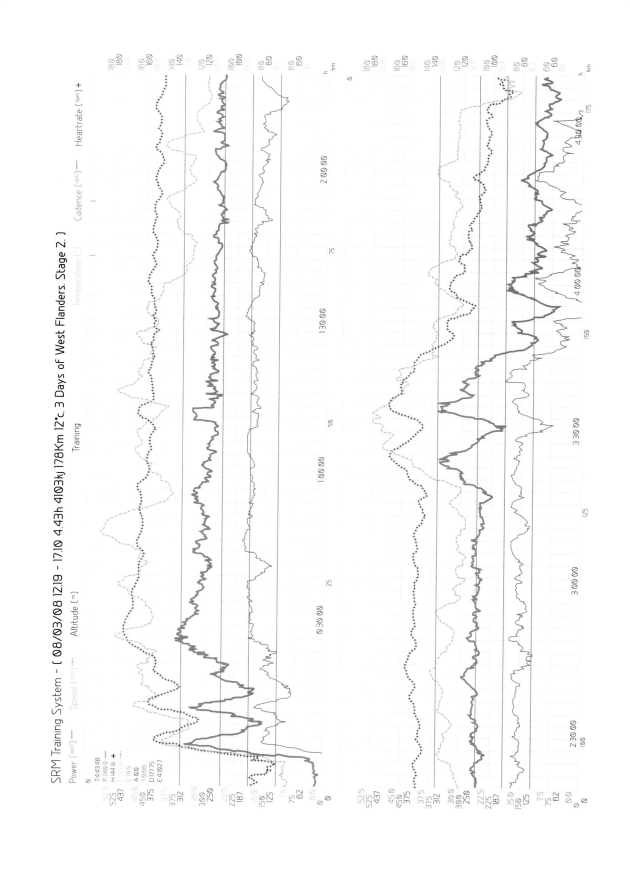

SRM Training System - [08/03/08 12.19 - 17.10 4.43h 4103kj 178Km 12°c. 3 Days of West Flanders. Stage 2.]

LEFT Strips of tape for earpieces of race radio.
Vuelta Ciclista al País Vasco. 2008

RIGHT Stepping off the bus.
Liège-Bastogne-Liège. 2008

OVERLEAF View from the observation tower at the Belvedere restaurant,
Mont Kemmelberg. Driedaagse van West - Vlaanderen. 2008

LEFT Saunier Duval merchandise at the stage I.
Vuelta Ciclista al País Vasco. 2008

RIGHT Saunier Duval merchandise at the stage II.
Vuelta Ciclista al País Vasco. 2008

FOREGROUND The feed station.
Driedaagse van West-Vlaanderen. 2008

Ronde van Vlaanderen, 2008

View from press car one minute before the peloton arrives, Paris–Roubaix, 2009

PREVIOUS PAGE: Views from the wall of Huy I. La Flèche Wallonne. 2008

Views from the wall of Huy II. La Flèche Wallonne. 2008

LEFT: Christophe Brandt finishing in the bitter cold at the top of the wall.
La Flèche Wallonne, 2008

RIGHT: Damiano Cunego winning in the bitter cold at the top of the wall.
Vuelta Ciclista al País Vasco, 2008

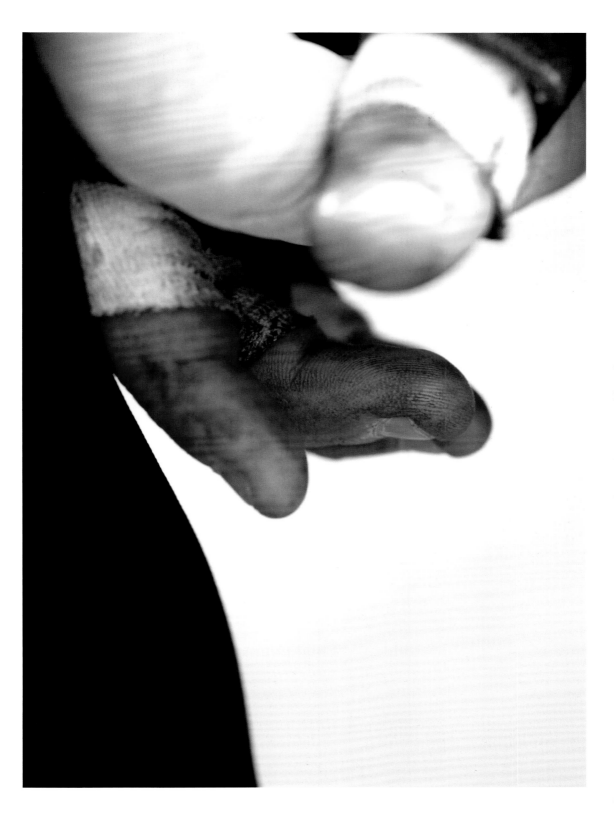

Finished rider II. Paris–Roubaix. 2009

Finished rider I. Paris–Roubaix. 2009

Hotel Vitoria-Gasteiz. Vuelta Ciclista al País Vasco. 2008

111

LEFT: View from team hotel. Vuelta Ciclista al País Vasco, 2008

RIGHT: Massage after the stage I. Hotel Kortrijk. Ronde van West-Vlaanderen, 2008

Massage after the stage II. Vuelta Ciclista al País Vasco. 2008

SUMMER

The effort is gauged. On the front of the peloton, which follows my wheel in a long single line, I set a pace that I can sustain for the required distance. My job is to catch the breakaway and to ride at an intensity uncomfortable enough that rivals in the peloton won't consider an attack. Behind, they're fighting for shelter from the wind as each rider tries to limit his effort. The road ahead is open. I pick the line the other 180 riders will follow and determine the speed at which we enter and accelerate out of the corners. The crowds spill into the road as we race over the hills. They jump to the roadside at the last moment as we speed towards them. On the front, I find a mental space that allows me to focus and while I do the job, the race becomes mine.

A hot wind blows from the left side. I ride on the right and leave just enough tarmac that the team can sit in my draft. Eight team-mates ride tightly behind, staggered to the right side of each other's rear wheel for maximum protection from the wind. Behind the last, the rest of the peloton rides in a long line on the few inches of road left before it crumbles into a grass ditch.

The last rider in the line of team-mates is Mark Cavendish, our team's sprinter, who will win.

The night before the race, lying on the hotel bed with my legs up, I page through the race book. Each rider is given one. It breaks down the three week race: stage by stage, kilometre by kilometre, and climb by climb. Alongside the maps and charts are photos of the towns we will race through, images of the peloton racing through the countryside, and portraits of the race's champions – the same champions whose photos I gazed at as a child. There are pages of rules, which I rarely read as they are the same in every race and have become a part of my life, like the traffic laws applied to a bus driver. I glance at the prize list but it is never something I focus on for long.

Every night for the three weeks I will open the book to study the next stage and its difficulties. Looking at the course profile in the book, I will become slightly nervous because of the unknown but will find comfort in the metered descriptions. Broken down the race seems humane; as a whole it seems absurd. The three Grand Tours – the Giro d'Italia, the Tour de France and the Vuelta a España – leave an impression on a rider's life. During the first Vuelta a España I rode, my team-mate David Zabriskie broke down in tears in the third week of the race as he fought to handle the stress of the workload. He cried like a boy and the directeur, Johan Bruyneel, struggled to comfort him like a father would have done.

With time our bodies become stronger, our minds accepting, and the challenge becomes one we can confront, although it is never painless. When a rider tells stories from a Grand Tour, his voice rises and he becomes animated like a student who has graduated from university. The accomplishment has an enduring impact on his life.

The champions in the photos of the race book look at ease on the bike. The sensation in my legs, as the muscles twitch, seems worlds away from those images of elegance. Yet I know that on the start line, I will have to accomplish a job regardless of the pain I feel and the requirement is that I push beyond it. Pain is something we learn to accept.

Cavendish sits beside me in his bed. He taps on his computer as he pulls up a video clip from the race he has just won. He seems to be moving incessantly. Even when he is sitting, his legs tap relentlessly. Like a pot boiling to the point of overflow, there is built-up energy or angst that seeps out slowly and is suddenly released in a rush as he sprints to the finish line. It is then that the energy becomes fury.

On the bed, he looks like any 20-year-old British boy. His shirtless torso doesn't evoke the power of a professional athlete. To the maid who comes to bring us new towels he must look like any other young adult – not the fastest, most victorious man in professional cycling. His skin is pasty and white; he is thin but not lean. He's short and stocky for a cyclist.

Electronic dance music beats from his computer's lousy speakers while he watches himself sprint in the clip. He analyses. Critiques. And then finds a surge of adrenaline, which has him suddenly up and dancing to the beat. He passes me the computer. "Watch this. It is fucking great." In the clip he destroys his rivals in a final violent surge towards the finish. His body is low on the bike and he grimaces with the pain of a man in a fight for his life. A primitive ferocity. "Watch the team. They're unbelievable." His childlike glee is in total contrast to the mouthy anger I have seen when he loses, or the focused professionalism he shows when zeroing in on a goal. With each change in his persona it is clear what makes him win with such frequency: passion, drive, and anger.

Watching the clip on his computer he knows how many metres each of his team-mates has pulled on the front for him. He respects their sacrifice. "I don't know how you guys do it. You're so fucking strong." Each rider in the team has a role, which is defined in the team meeting prior to the race. As we develop a bond of respect and become a tight team, there is a mutual understanding and we each assume our roles.

The races never leave our lives. We sleep with them. We wake up to them. We live them in each of our movements and thoughts.

Beside his bed, his suitcase is open. His clothing is neatly folded. He has meticulously prepared as if the details of what he carries will affect his performance. To him, they will. Everything is ready the night before the start. He cleans his shoes with the care a tailor gives to a bespoke suit. The only things left undone are his numbers, which are placed on his neatly folded jersey but not yet pinned. They won't go on until we are on our way to the start in the team bus. He has told me: "Don't pin your numbers on the night before. It's bad luck." We all want to control what we can't. Superstition is the result of fear. As a daily ritual, we pin on our numbers and each rider pins them differently in a style learned as a young cyclist. We develop habits that stay with us through our careers.

I gaze at the folded jersey. It is now mostly a uniform. As an amateur, a professional jersey was something that held a dream. Those bought or given to me were cherished even though they didn't have the weight of a real professional *maillot*. In a jersey, there was a vision of glamour: the colours, the logos, the uniformity. The image it held was one of fancy cars, big homes, fine hotels and a life of fame, comfort and luxury. The riders who wore them were professionals. They were my idols.

Christian Vande Velde, who had the same dream, told me that as a child he believed that professionals didn't even have to pin on their own numbers, as that was the soigneur's job. We all had our own ideals. During his first season he was shocked at the realities of our life: the dirty hotels, the riders who raced for wages below the poverty line, and the hours spent suffering on a wheel in cold rain with no hope of ever seeing the front of the race. Soon, those realities were accepted but, even then, the dream never faded completely.

No longer do professionals wash their clothing in their rooms as riders did a decade ago. Spoiled, our clothing is cleaned daily by the soigneurs in the team truck and returned to us at breakfast in the morning. A jersey lasts a month. They fade with the sun and stain with rain while the seams wear and give out. Only when I pull it over my head and see my body in a mirror do I feel a flutter of pride and accomplishment. Then, it is off to work.

While chasing the breakaway, we focus solely on the pursuit and capture, while the riders ahead play a tactical game as they try to conserve energy in case they do make it to within reach of the finish ahead of the peloton – then they'll need the saved energy to sprint each other for the victory. A director will always tell a rider in the breakaway to do less than the rider who is doing the least work.

By committing to the chase and the team, I have sacrificed any hope of a personal result, which allows me to give everything to the pursuit. During my first season with the US Postal Service, Lance Armstrong's team, I was taught how to ride for the leader. The team was built around him and his goal was to win the Tour de France. They hired a squad of domestiques who were talented enough to win alone but who would always ride for the leader.

As team-mates and rival teams with the same ambitions begin to ride with me in a paceline to increase the tempo, the rhythm changes. My rhythm changes. The speed of the peloton fluctuates as different riders drive the pursuit in their own manner. Some ride to show off for the television audience while others, unable to find a consistent pace, surge and slow. Riding alone, my legs sustain a consistent pressure, as a driver might apply his foot to the accelerator on a highway. Riding in a paceline with others, sharing the effort, I feel a surge and release of muscular stress and pressure. As my body is hit by the wind when it is my turn to ride on the front, my leg muscles tighten, my body drops lower, and my breathing increases. As my turn ends and I pull off the front, there is an almost mechanical release as I jump back into the draft. On the front my breath is intense and deep; while sitting in the wheels I can sit up, stretch, eat or drink. Our efforts in the wind within the paceline are dosed by distance, speed and effort. We pull long enough to tow the line, short enough to maintain the speed, and steady enough not to break the rhythm. Sharp accelerations, or surges, do more harm than good as they fracture the line, which works with the momentum of a metronome. The paceline can work with fluidity as each rider pedals a steady cadence that sets the speed of the rotating paceline. In synch, the chase group flows with a unique beauty.

As we take turns, each riding a few minutes in the wind, we develop a bond in the shared effort. Rivals become team-mates as we have a common goal in our pursuit of the breakaway. Food and drinks are shared. Obstacles on the course are pointed out. The consistent tempo is the essence; we cooperate to ensure the rhythm is maintained.

With each passing kilometre I become more comfortable in the arched aerodynamic position I bend into while I ride on the front in the wind. During the first days where hours are spent riding in the tight form, my back, hips, neck and arms ache. When there is a momentary lull, a descent, or a technical bit of course, I sit up and stretch like a cat preparing to attack, before falling back into my compact form. Through the days, my body adapts to the low aerodynamic position, my muscles strengthen, and I begin to feel awkward sitting up on my bike like a postman.

On the front with the same domestiques, I can discover their weaknesses and strengths. As we grow tired in the pursuit, it becomes evident when their bodies begin to give in. I will have ridden in a steady paceline with two to ten other riders, often the same ones, for hours every day. In those hours I watch their movement on a bike like a psychiatrist eyes the patient. I begin to see when another rider's body is going to fail and they only have a few more turns on the front left in their legs before they fade into the peloton and eventually off the back. Like a candlewick that is slowly flickering before it is absorbed by the wax it has melted, their pulls become shorter and slower. Their effort fades with their desire. Their legs, which look solid as trunks at the start of the day, begin to falter like twigs.

In the peloton there is a shared intimacy, which is unlike that of any other social environment. In the massive flowing bunch, we place trust in the riders around us. Descending a mountain at 90 km/h we follow the line, placing blind faith that the abilities on the bike of the riders in front are honed, their awareness is acute, and they are considering the others who follow as they corner at speed. Our lives are dependent on each other – a misjudged corner, a hit pothole, or an erratic movement is potentially lethal.

Riders blow their noses; we spit and we sweat. It all flies within the peloton, commonplace and unavoidable. With our mouths open to suck in air and our eyes vigilant of the road ahead, we're saturated by dirty rainwater – often from manure-covered farm roads – that sprays from the tyres. The peloton is in the battle together; we accept the abnormalities to reach the line. And we fall ill together. Often, viruses spread through the entire peloton within days. Our immune systems are weakened by the stress of the race and we fall ill easily. The team environment is tight – we eat, sleep and travel together. Our stomachs become our weakest point as we swallow thousands of calories

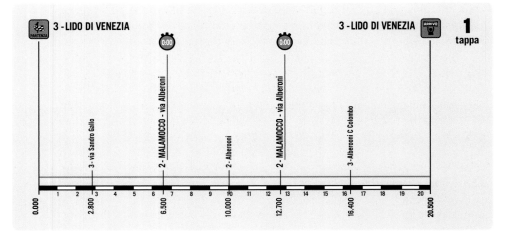

3 - LIDO DI VENEZIA (PARTENZA)
3 - LIDO DI VENEZIA (ARRIVO)
1 tappa

0:00 — 0:00

- 3 - via Sandro Gallo
- 2 - MALAMOCCO - via Alberoni
- 2 - Alberoni
- 2 - MALAMOCCO - via Alberoni
- 3 - Alberoni C Colombo

0.000 | 1 | 2 | 2.800 | 3 | 4 | 5 | 6 | 6.500 | 7 | 8 | 9 | 10.000 | 10 | 11 | 12 | 12.700 | 13 | 14 | 15 | 16 | 16.400 | 17 | 18 | 19 | 20 | 20.500

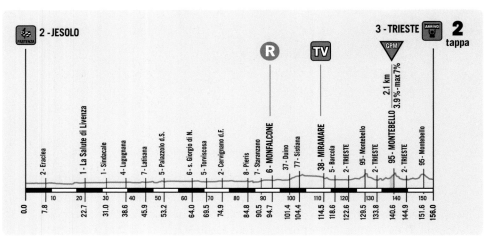

2 - JESOLO (PARTENZA)
3 - TRIESTE (ARRIVO)
2 tappa

R — TV — GPM

2,1 km
3,9% - max 7%

- 2 - Eraclea
- 1 - La Salute di Livenza
- 1 - Sindacale
- 4 - Lugugnana
- 7 - Latisana
- 5 - Palazzolo d.S.
- 6 - s. Giorgio di N.
- 5 - Torviscosa
- 2 - Cervignano d.F.
- 8 - Pieris
- 7 - Staranzano
- 6 - MONFALCONE
- 37 - Duino
- 77 - Sistiana
- 38 - MIRAMARE
- 5 - Barcola
- 2 - TRIESTE
- 95 - Montebello
- 2 - TRIESTE
- 95 - MONTEBELLO
- 2 - TRIESTE
- 95 - Montebello

0.0 | 7.8 | 10 | 20 | 22.7 | 31.0 | 30 | 38.6 | 40 | 45.9 | 50 | 53.2 | 60 | 64.0 | 69.5 | 74.9 | 80 | 84.8 | 90.5 | 94.7 | 90 | 101.4 | 104.4 | 100 | 114.5 | 110 | 118.6 | 122.6 | 120 | 129.5 | 130 | 133.8 | 140.6 | 140 | 144.9 | 151.6 | 150 | 156.0

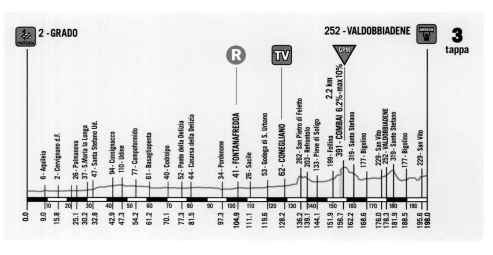

2 - GRADO (PARTENZA)
252 - VALDOBBIADENE (ARRIVO)
3 tappa

R — TV — GPM

2,2 km
6,2% - max 10%

- 6 - Aquileia
- 2 - Cervignano d.F.
- 26 - Palmanova
- 37 - S.Maria la Longa
- 47 - Santa Stefano Ud.
- 94 - Cussignacco
- 110 - Udine
- 77 - Campoformido
- 61 - Basagliapenta
- 40 - Codroipo
- 52 - Ponte della Delizia
- 44 - Casarsa della Delizia
- 34 - Pordenone
- 41 - FONTANAFREDDA
- 26 - Sacile
- 53 - Godega di S. Urbano
- 62 - CONEGLIANO
- 262 - San Pietro di Feletto
- 203 - Refrontolo
- 133 - Pieve di Soligo
- 199 - Follina
- 391 - COMBAI
- 319 - Santo Stefano
- 177 - Bigolino
- 229 - San Vito
- 252 - VALDOBBIADENE
- 319 - Santo Stefano
- 177 - Bigolino
- 229 - San Vito

0.0 | 9.0 | 10 | 15.8 | 20 | 25.1 | 30.2 | 32.8 | 30 | 42.9 | 47.3 | 40 | 54.2 | 50 | 61.2 | 70.1 | 60 | 77.3 | 81.5 | 70 | 80 | 97.3 | 90 | 104.9 | 100 | 111.1 | 110 | 119.6 | 128.2 | 120 | 136.2 | 139.1 | 130 | 144.1 | 140 | 151.9 | 156.7 | 150 | 162.2 | 160 | 168.6 | 170 | 176.0 | 181.3 | 180 | 188.9 | 188.5 | 190 | 195.6 | 198.0

of food a day and push through litres of fluid. If our legs are the pistons, our stomachs are the motors and in a stage race both are worked to their limit. The motor is pumped with fuel so the pistons can pound out 90 revolutions per minute for five to seven hours. When the pistons are damaged, we pump in more fuel in the hope they can recover in time for the next pounding.

The television motorcycle drives metres in front of us, or alongside, as it buzzes around the front of the peloton to find a spot where the cameraman can catch the best images without impeding the race. The cars, motorcycles, cyclists and fans that make up the race use every metre of the road. I focus on the metres that concern me as I choose the quickest, safest line avoiding potholes and grit. Occasionally, I will surge to momentarily catch the motorcycle's draft before it revs ahead. We seek any small advantage that will make the race easier and shorter.

Riders who have friends on the motorbikes or in cars take advantage of the relationship and draft whenever they are out of sight of the cameras and commissaires – races have been won because of the draft of a vehicle. National pride also transcends ethics as drivers help riders simply because of their nationality or their idolatry.

Soon after the breakaway is established, teams form a paceline on the front and the pace remains high and steady. The peloton is a long thin line, stretching out over the countryside and winding through villages. The moments during the race where we can relax to stop for a pee are few; time lost to the breakaway leaves more work. The goal for our team is to bring back the breakaway so that Mark Cavendish can win the stage.

Midway through a three week stage race, wear begins to show in the peloton. Riders who looked smooth on their bikes in the first days of the race seem uncomfortable in the paceline. Their efforts on the front are less potent and their surges to slide back into the group panicked. Their pedal strokes become laboured. They readjust their positions repeatedly in the hope that a change might ease the pain; like a horse that has been running for too long and too fast, there is an awkwardness that appears when muscles begin to fail.

Gaps in the once fluid mass of a peloton open quickly when the wind blows at our side or there is a harsh acceleration. Tempers flare as tired riders can no longer handle the normal stress of the race.

As I ride on the front the peloton behind isn't my focus, or even a concern. The goal is ahead, on the road and at the finish. To complete the task I must find comfort in the effort and to do that, I forget about everything else. The kilometres pass. The odometer counts them off. The race is broken down; the effort becomes manageable. There are 160 kilometres until the finish. The breakaway needs to be caught before the last ten. My effort will last for a minimum of 150 kilometres, or just over three hours. We gauge our progress on time gaps which are relayed to us over the race radio, or by the times scribbled on a chalkboard held by a commissaire who rides on the back of a motorcycle.

For those at the back of the peloton, the race is exponentially harder. I have been there many times when my morale was low and my legs were empty. Ironically, those who don't have the fight left to be up front are doing more work, as the peloton is elastic – it whips with speed at the tail end as we accelerate out of corners or up mountains. Seeing 200 riders ahead sprinting out of a corner while waiting, virtually standing still, for the bottleneck before me to clear is unsettling as I know that within seconds I will be riding with every watt of energy in my legs to maintain the distance to the wheel in front of me. We will spin out our largest gear with our noses on our stems, crouching to become more aerodynamic and hoping the next acceleration won't throttle us as violently. On a bad day, there can be dozens of painful moments before the elastic eventually snaps and the rider is left alone, in the wind, as the peloton speeds away into the distance.

As I ride on the front, tapping out my tempo, long straight roads melt in the heat and the horizon is a blur of spectators, motorbikes, cars, fumes, buildings and sunlight. I look down at my handlebars, my bottle, my grit-covered sweat-glistening shins and knees. I watch them turn for a moment then look up again into the blur of heat. A motorcycle zooms up, a photographer snaps a photo and speeds away. Nothing seems to be moving quickly ahead of me; it appears to be melting. I reach down, grab my bottle, sip, and douse my head with water. In the 40 minutes the bottle has been on my bike, the water now tastes like plastic and has the temperature of bath water.

Spectators' cheers are muted. They stand under umbrellas sipping drinks in their swimsuits with sun hats shading their faces. The heat has suffocated their usual ebullience. Nobody wants to be out on a day so warm that black tarmac burns bare feet.

The warmth melts our bodies. The riders I work with on the front become thinner as their bodies sweat out litres of water every hour. The body pushes out salt as it works to maintain balanced levels to avoid toxicity, and the shorts and jerseys turn white with crystallised salt. Drops of sweat sting our eyes, blinding us momentarily.

For some the heat stifles their performance, as their bodies are unable to perform under the added stress. Their muscles cramp, they can't eat to fuel themselves, and they wilt, becoming thin and gaunt as the race progresses. The heat saps the potency they woke up with in the morning. Others adapt quickly and reach their peaks in the scorching sun. Generally, those who suffer in the heat were born in northern, cooler climates, while those who fly are Spaniards, Portuguese, South Americans or from southern Italy.

With an hour left to race the peloton slowly becomes a mass again as each team rides near the front in our slipstream. No longer in a single line, the peloton uses every inch of road behind the arrow we create at the front of the bubble. I sense the surge in speed over my shoulders. Their energy is intense. I can feel their panic as they push and shove to stay at the front without wasting too much energy. *Profiteurs*. The bubble they create behind me is chaotic and I am happy to be increasing the speed on the front, giving it everything I have while staying out of the mess behind. I hear screeching brakes, skidding tyres and yells. Knowing my team-mates are okay, I ignore the noise and press on.

Through our earpieces, the directeur sportif encourages us with increasing fervour as we close on the finish. What begins as short directives and occasional time checks becomes panicked emotional yells as he tries to put his energy into our pedals. From the car behind he can only see a small window of what is our experience. His emotions are drawn from his past experience on the bike – they always forget the pain – and the images he can see on the small television screen in the car. Sometimes the encouragement works while often it simply annoys and frustrates. Experience has given us the knowledge we need; motivation is not found in panic or abuse.

As the team lines up for the finale, the last 20 kilometres, everything seems possible. From the front we are in complete control. Cavendish, sitting tightly in the team's draft, pushes riders who challenge him for his prime position and fight for it, bouncing off his elbows like bumper cars off the barriers. His bike barely moves with each hit. Out of the draft, his attackers are unable to hold the position and fade away into the wheels behind.

In the last few minutes of five hours on the bike, the race reaches a crescendo. As a symphony progresses to the emotional moment where everything culminates, the peloton has orchestrated the same result. In the finale, the peloton is alight in its chaos, the television audience sits on edge, and the roadside spectators crane over the barriers to scream at their heroes. The tedious predictable pursuit evolves into wild chaotic fury. Riders crash, scream, and yell. Others cuss as riders hit each other in the fight for the front. Shoes clip wheels, pedals clip corners, arms touch arms, and hips push against hips. The peloton, like a torrent running wild down a gorge, is a mass with thousands of different movements within.

But with clarity and calm, a rider can see the movements, predict them and react to them to avoid disaster. In panic nothing is clear, as a rider will only see the wheel in front, and he will lose energy and focus, and, at worst, crash. Victories build confidence and confidence reduces panic, which results in more victories.

In the final surge towards the line everything becomes a blur. My eyes begin to water with the effort and the increased speed. Through the smudges of salty sweat that cloud my sunglasses, I drive the peloton for the last metres. My team-mates yell encouragement behind me. As I force in litres of oxygen, the effort is so intense that I can't speak a word. Comfortable in my draft the team is in control behind me. Within seconds they will feel the same pain. As I pull over, my work finished and my body wasted, they'll take the lead at the head of the charging peloton in turn. Each rider will pedal with a ferocity that will leave his body spent before the finish line is reached. Our goal is to launch Cavendish into his sprint for the line at the highest possible speed while keeping all of his rivals behind.

The team rides in the same tight formation it has been in since the first hour of the race, but now we are reaching our maximum speed. We fly through the city streets well above speed limits. The team tears through corners, gauging

COLUMBIA - HIGH ROAD

AREE ACCESSIBILI

INVITATO ATLETA

the trajectory to the centimetre as we accelerate alongside the barriers and launch out, our speed blowing the promotional hats from the spectators' heads. The closer to the finish line, the shorter, fiercer and faster we ride.

As each of us completes our effort, we quickly move away from the head of the peloton, pulling to the side of the road and decelerating like a dragster slows when its parachute pops. Yet there is no need to touch the brakes to slow as our bodies simply shut down, unable to pedal any further. We coast as the sprinters charge for the line. We listen to the announcer over the loudspeakers and the directeur over the race radio for the result. The lactic acid sears our muscles as we slowly breathe in and out to recover. Riders speed past. We are unconcerned with our personal result: Cavendish's victory is all that matters – we crane to see the head of the peloton as the sprinters cross the line. And then, knowing he has won, my body is covered in goose pimples. The job is done. There is a sense of relief and also a sense of accomplishment. Controlling the race is a thrill and for brief moment I feel on top of the world.

Reaching the finish I look for the moving mass of people. The blacks, greys and beiges of the media contrast with the sharp colours of Cavendish's team clothing. He rides slowly amidst the mass that moves with him. As our bodies seek calm, the journalists spring into action. Voices from the crowd cheer congratulations. Journalists pat my back as they race toward the crowd. The team pushes through the mass of pushing people. Annoyed and in haste, Cavendish pushes away the cameras. The crowd creates a feeling of claustrophobia in the intense heat. Realising they have another photo opportunity, they step back from his side as he embraces us each. With sincerity he hugs us tight. Our bodies still shudder from the effort and our clothing is soaked with sweat. Around us the buzz is intense but in that moment I see none of it – in that moment we are a team together. The cheers of the crowds and the throng of media attention are suddenly insignificant as they are transcended by the emotion of completion and contentment. The magnificently executed team effort is the essence of my elation.

Cavendish became the most victorious rider in the peloton because he gained confidence through the efforts of his team-mates and his victories, and in turn the effectiveness of the team grew. Our confidence swelled with each of the victories and we learned to control the peloton over any race course that could end in a sprint. Rivals waited for us to lead the pursuit in the hopes that we would tire. Ironically, a team must ride from the front and control every situation to win repeatedly.

Twenty-year-old sportsmen should not be responsible for carrying the pressure born from a legion of fans, rivals, and managers who only care about the end result. They're too young. They're still immature boys who haven't learned how to live away from their parents' home. Mark's phone rings repeatedly through the day. Rarely does he answer immediately. He told me once: "I never wanted all of this. I only wanted to ride my bike."

On his bike, his personality flips. The thoughtful boy becomes a focused, fiery competitor. He analyses his competition and builds his strength by finding their errors: he notices their fluidity on the bike, their weight, and their position in the peloton. Whatever fault he finds, he uses it as his fuel. In the race, when he is expected to win, he is virtually unapproachable. On the bike, he sits confidently with an air of arrogance as his nose is held high and his head slightly up. Like a basketball player struts onto the court with his hair freshly cut, his shoes brand new and his shorts just so, Cavendish will have carefully selected his glasses from the dozens in his bag, chosen his shoes and made sure his team clothing is perfect for the day. It is a game of intimidation.

Terse and loud he barks directives and orders at his team-mates. We tell him to calm down or we simply ignore the voice, knowing it is because of the pressure he has placed on himself, and follow through with the task.

When we are not pulling on the front to set him up for the victory, we are taking care of him in the peloton to ensure he saves energy. In my first year as a professional in Europe, I was told by our directeur, Bruyneel, how to ride for a leader: "You stay at his side until you need to get something for him from the car. Always. He stops to pee, you stop to pee. He needs a jacket you get it quickly and return to his side. Your job is to help him, keep him out of the wind, until you can no longer pedal properly." Every watt of energy saved can make the difference between winning and losing. The domestique's sacrifice is what makes a champion and the champions have always trusted domestiques.

"What the public…" Mark stops mid-sentence to correct himself. "No, no, not only the public." He restarts his statement. "What most cycling enthusiasts don't understand is that I never have easy days. If the stage is flat, or even undulating, I need to be ready to sprint. If there are mountains, I need to suffer like a fucking dog to get to the finish within the time cut, and when I ride a time trial, I am either there to go for the victory – if it is short enough – or I just hold on to make the time cut. People think we are fucking lazy – that we depend on the team and only accelerate in the last metres. I get to the room completely dead every night. When all the climbers rejoice that the stage is flat and they can recover, I need to amp myself up. I can't relax. Ever."

Cavendish, like all of the sprinters with their muscular bodies, struggles in the mountains where power-to-weight determines the speed at which a rider can climb. And he suffers.

When Mark can't win a stage because of the undulating terrain, we, his domestiques, ride with him tight in our draft off the back of the peloton. Days, even weeks, pass where it seems as though I am either on the front or off the back of the peloton, relentlessly pulling in the wind regardless of my position in the race. The race off the back of the peloton is a steady, persistent effort against the clock as we must finish within the time limit imposed by the race organiser: usually within 14 per cent of the winner's time on a hard mountainous stage. A second team directeur sportif, who follows us well behind the leaders, encourages us in the same way the directeur in the first team car supports the climber. He keeps us fed, hydrated and informed, telling us how long the climbs are, how far we have until the finish, and how much time we have until we are excluded from the race for being outside the time cut.

From the start of the mountain stage, I remain with Mark, keeping him in front at the bottom of the climbs so he can slowly drift back through the long peloton in the hope that at the top he is still in contact with the group or close enough to catch up on the descent. To avoid panicked pursuits of the attacking peloton, our energy expenditures are calibrated. Like a car running with a near empty tank, accelerations drain energy needlessly and can end in ruin. We ride at a steady, sustainable speed.

On the climbs, Mark needs to go hard enough to remain in contact until we are close enough to the finish that he can comfortably arrive within the time cut without sapping all of his energy for the coming days. More comfortable than him on the climbs, it is on the flats and descents where I feel the effort. This is where we need to chase like savages to maintain a reasonable time gap.

Behind the race, rivals cooperate to make it to the finish in the gruppettos – the small packs of dropped riders that pool together. We will work with our fiercest rivals in a tight echelon to make it to the finish. Solidarity develops in the struggle to make it within the time cut: our race becomes one of simple survival. Each rider has a common goal and together it is easier to achieve that goal – alone it is virtually impossible. In the gruppettos, the domestiques still do the load of the work, as they know that every metre a leader pulls in the wind will make the difference when he is the one who has the chance to win.

In the gruppettos, it is evident which riders will not make it to the finish in the coming stages. Their bodies sway on their bikes, their faces look worn, they can no longer pull in the wind, they open gaps in the group repeatedly, and they have lost all of their morale to race. At dinner each night, my US Postal team-mate Benoît Joachim would run down the results page and list the riders he predicted would be home before the tour was over. Each rider he saw in rough-looking shape, he added to his 'a la casa' list (riders he thought wouldn't make it through the race and would be home soon due to poor fitness). His daily predictions were always correct which was either a sign that he was abnormally perceptive or that he was too often near the back of the peloton.

But even on their worst days, some riders never change. They may lack the coup de pédale to win yet their torsos never sway with fatigue. Their bodies seem to be built on their bikes. Their stems are low, their saddles high, their backs flat and their pedal stroke fluid. On all terrain, at every speed, they look the same: strong. They pierce through the air, turning the pedals while the rest of the body remains motionless. In form, they look beautiful as the grimace of emotion from the effort tells a story that their bodies mask. A fury roars inside but the exterior of the plane appears quietly serene.

Francesco Moser, the Italian champion who won on the cobbles and in the mountains, looked as if he was born on his bike. As a child I gazed at photos of him and watched him in old videos, his arms absorbing the cobbles like a car's suspension and making the cobbled road appear smooth beneath his bike and body. Everything seemed to fit together; he looked as if he was born for that moment. Hours of riding cannot give a human that elegance.

Some Eastern European riders, and most notably the Russians, look as if they have been caned into their positions. Their torsos are motionless on their bikes as they pedal out a mechanical stroke. They look smooth yet controlled in the same way a programmed song can have all of the right elements, but never be a hit.

In the images of the sprint finishes, Mark's position on the bike contrasts that of his rivals – you can see the mass of riders charging the line, all sitting high on their bikes, with one rider who is roughly a foot lower. Traditionally, sprinters sit high on their bikes, as they pull up on the handlebars to push power into their pedals. Mark seems to do the opposite – by sitting low and forward he pushes into the bars forcing his weight forward. Tucked into a tight ball his compact torso becomes even smaller and his legs spin a massive gear beneath. Through the decades, riders have adapted and their positions have evolved to find speed. We still do the same thing as the riders who rode the Classics and Tours decades ago, but we do it differently: competition breeds evolution.

To beat his rivals, Mark's position – perhaps subconsciously – evolved so that he could win. That change in position will slowly become the norm within the peloton as the next generation of riders will ape his style while his current rivals, who are astute enough, will adopt it to match Mark's speed. Athletes seek out the minute details to make up, or forge, the gap. Position is no less critical than equipment, diet, vitamins, training techniques and, for some, medicine.

With the increase in budgets within the peloton, many teams now have the resources to seek out the advantages that make the difference while other teams, stuck in a rut by dreaming of past glory, remain steadfast that the traditional methods are the best. In the last quarter of the 20th century, it was the foreign riders who forced change with their open mentality to the three main aspects that affect performance: training, diet and equipment. Most Europeans, who had dominated the races for most of the century, were scared to evolve. They had their formula for victory and were adamant that it was the only way to race a bike. Slowly, they have adapted as methods were proven to improve performance and they were repeatedly beaten in the races they once commanded and won.

Innovation has also taken away from cycling. The two-way radios that tether us to the team directeur sportif driving behind the peloton have dulled the event by muting the riders' instincts and creating formulaic and predictable racing. The short directives barked over the radio from the directeur sportif become the final word and most riders will follow every order instead of using their knowledge of the race, the course and their bodies to determine the outcome. The first teams to use the radios had a clear advantage over those who didn't as they could orchestrate their movements in the peloton quickly. As the radios are now ubiquitous in the bunch, the advantage is gone and they simply cause panic, chaos and danger as 20 directeurs yell commands at the same moment. Instantaneously, there is a surge and 200 riders are racing for the front. The event becomes dangerous and scripted as the variables that make racing challenging and exciting are simplified and even eliminated. The greatest champions won not only because they were physically gifted but also because they could read and feel the race.

Christian Rumeau directed teams in an era before radios commanded the race. He had a feel for the race, unlike many of the modern directeurs who have become dependent on the technology. Rumeau could look in a rider's eyes and see if he was ready to perform or needed to rest. He cared in a motherly way; he seemed to watch every pedal stroke. Most modern cycling team management is more worried with the end result in the same way most doctors treat their patients. Cycling has become clinical.

In mid-June, the Tour de France selection begins to fracture teams who promote competition within to decide rosters; team-mates will race against each other to prove they deserve their spot, to the detriment of the whole. Directeurs, too naive to see the damage it does to the team, encourage the competition by postponing the selection and by giving false hope to riders with little chance of making it to the start. Inevitably some riders feel soured by the experience. Directeurs who have fallen into the hierarchical structure that dominates most teams often aren't the best managers or teachers but become dictators, as they feel threatened and struggle with honesty.

Dynamics within teams are often contentious as directeurs, most of whom were once professionals, often use their careers to judge the riders they coach. To race as a professional, you need to forget the hard moments to survive and persist. Directeurs often make decisions based on their memories, which are skewed. With time we forget the pain we feel in our legs and the anguish when we are dropped from the peloton. It is the victories, the vicious acceleration and other glorious moments we embrace and remember. Directeurs, unhappy with their own careers on the bike, develop jealousies based in their insecurities. Riders who were hard workers, who fought on the bike, who enjoyed *'le métier'*, who rode not for the money or glory but for the love, make the best directeurs as they have respect for the rider and his effort. A team with a nurturing environment will be able to maximise an individual's potential.

With a good team, an individual can push his body further as the morale of the group lifts his performance. Humans perform in packs, as our primitive instincts push us to conform, to be a part of the group, to contribute, and to achieve for the benefit of the whole. Together cyclists suffer to extremes as the mental can overcome the physical: we suppress the pain to avoid failing the team.

Unlike in most other team sports, where roles are clearly defined and it is the team that is congratulated for the victory rather than the individual, we are often alone in our effort. When we perform, the team rises; when we fail, we are alone in that failure. Personal defeat isn't shared – on a field with other team-mates, failures fall on the team, whereas we are isolated and struggle alone on a bike. Dropped from the group, we ride alone on the road as the peloton speeds away. This is the emptiest moment in a cyclist's life: no longer able to hold onto the last wheel in the bunch, the gap grows, the team cars speed past, and there is suddenly an abandoned sense of silence. He now hears only his chain meshing with the sprockets, his breath, and the surrounding environment. He is no longer playing in the show. He is no longer a member of the pack. Questions arise in his head. Tears form in his eyes. He has sacrificed normal life for cycling for years. The loss is significant.

The time trial is the ultimate solitary test on a bike. During the individual race we can't slide into a slipstream to recover. There are no team-mates to rely on, or any others off whom we can gauge the effort. It is simply the cyclist on the open road against a clock. For this, the time trial has been known as the race of truth.

I try to isolate myself from the world around me by losing my thoughts in my music and the rhythm of my pedal stroke. The hometrainer on which I warm up for the individual time trial is placed beside the team bus. The bus's motor churns, revs and spews beside me as it cools the interior where my team-mates climb into their gear and seclude themselves from the spectators who buzz around outside. Above me, the awning that shades the warming up riders from the scorching sun does little to keep me cool. Sweat drips down my face, drop by drop, soaking me slowly as my intensity increases with my cadence. My body drops on the bike and finds the position where I can produce consistent power. The beat of the music increases and my cadence quickens. Fans watch closely – most know not to disturb us with requests for photos or autographs. The intensity on our faces likely tells them that this is not the moment. I think of the course, the corners, the climbs, and the effort I will produce alone on the road – a consistent, focused effort is all I need. I close my eyes and envision my past and my future.

My leg speed increases. I open my eyes glancing briefly at the cranks and my feet as they spin. My legs don't feel a part of my body but more a piece of the machine. Riding, nothing has changed; as I sit on the bike, I feel as I did as a child in the garage, pounding out a beat on my pedals as the music blasted into my ears. In intense symbiosis, my bicycle becomes an extension of my body. The machine moves with fluidity.

On the course, which I have ridden and memorised, I push my body into a place where the intensity of the effort becomes a part of the machine. If I go beyond that, I will come to pieces – when I lose the balance and overextend, corners are misjudged, my pedal stroke loses its potent fluidity, and I am unable to sustain the effort. Like the bicycle I ride, my body and mind become mechanical and only in the finale do I push to my maximum. At that moment, it no longer matters whether or not the motor explodes under the pressure.

In the last kilometres of the race, when the finish is nearly in sight, I will rip myself to pieces. My lungs will burn and my legs will be unable to support me after I cross the line. I will taste blood and cough from the dry hot air pumping in and out at an abnormal rate. In those final kilometres, the crowds will become a blur as my eyes water and my mind loses focus of everything but the finishing banner. The signs counting down the metres left until I reach the line will seem increasingly far apart as each stroke my legs pound out increases the lactic acid and sensation of burning pain. I try to block that pain out and push beyond it. There are only metres to go. I cross the line. I am shattered. Empty, I coast. My arms are weak, my hands shake and my legs can no longer turn in circles. I try to slow everything down and refocus. A deep breath. Another. In haste, I pull off my helmet and glasses, which are dripping with sweat and white with salt, as they give me a feeling of claustrophobia. I unzip my tight skinsuit. My body needs to breathe. The effort has pushed the world out of focus and has consumed me. Slowly, I re-enter.

I reach the bus. A soigneur grabs hold of me and helps me off my bike. The spectators move away to allow me through the crowd and into the bus. A mechanic takes my bike from me and pats me on the back. He congratulates me – not for the result but for the effort. I won't see the specialised time trial bike he tucks away in the back of the truck until the next event I ride. Its top tube is covered in mucus and sweat, as are my thighs and arms. Clearing my airways during the race, I blew my nose repeatedly, primitively. My legs feel weak and empty as I climb the stairs onto the bus. My extremities shake slightly as my heart continues to race, pumping litres of blood to recover.

The bus is now quiet inside as my team-mates are either out on the course or back at the hotel. Jackets hang from chairs, jerseys lie amongst piles of wet clothing, and headphones continue to bleat out music as the players sit on the seats, abandoned in the rush to the start line. Like a classroom vacated by students for recess, there is calm in the bus but also a sense of the noise and rush of minutes prior.

As I sit in the leather chair, my legs soaking it with sweat, my body finally returns to its normal rhythm. I sip on a bottle of water and look up at the television as riders on the screen cross the line, one by one. Their times are posted. I glance and look away as I know I have done my best – I will see where I stack up later. For now, I need to breathe. If beaten, I will question and analyse every detail of the race. And then forget about it and move on.

In the race of truth, technology plays a greater role than on the road where aerodynamics is less consequential due to drafting. The bike, the wheels, the clothing, the helmet and, most importantly, the rider's position make massive differences in an individual event. Teams with the best equipment will consistently place their entire team at the top of the rankings. The riders aren't necessarily better time trialists, or physically stronger, but they have arrived with the best equipment for the event.

And while it's always been called the race of truth, it has slowly become a test of technology as teams seek even the most marginal of gains. Team budgets and infrastructure transcend an individual's potential as the teams with resources and know-how gain the advantage. Riders now depend on radio communication during the time trial to pace themselves and to know where they stack up against the competition as the directeur follows the race over a live television feed in the team car, relaying the important details to the rider. No longer is performance pure in the way the solo effort was originally intended. But, regardless, there is nowhere to hide when you are out on the road, alone in the wind. There are no wheels to follow and no drafts in which to hide. The effort is mentally and physically draining.

I descend from the bus, my tight fit skinsuit tucked around my waist, and my torso still sweating. I pull on an undervest, climb back on my bike that sits on the trainer, and begin to pedal again. My legs have lost all of the energy they had only an hour prior. They are weak and barely able to pedal. I find a gear that is comfortable to push, not straining my legs. The soigneur chats with me about the race, gives me a towel to dry the sweat and a bottle to rehydrate.

He is a caregiver. The soigneurs are relentlessly working for us. They nurse us back from injury, keep us fed and hydrated, ensure our muscles are ready to perform and that we only have our race to worry about. Their job begins before dawn and ends long after we're asleep. They drive the team cars across Europe. They prepare sandwiches for the next day while we sit in our rooms with our legs in the air. Their lives, like ours, are ones of routine. While cyclists need to be self-focused to ensure performance, their lives are devoted to others. Their routine is one in which they constantly give and rarely receive. The best soigneurs are those with a passion for cycling – they take pride in their jobs and rejoice in our victories. Like anyone working within professional cycling, they need to love the bike to survive, as without that love the sacrifice is too great.

Back at the hotel, my body is recovering from the effort. The food I have eaten after the race is slowly replenishing my body. On the massage table, the soigneur strokes out the knots that have developed in my muscles. He works at them, like a baker kneading his dough, until the muscle is again fluid and soft. Like the cyclists on the team, with diversity in culture and training, each soigneur has developed unique techniques with time and experience. Some are educated in massage while others have simply learned their skills from others and from having their legs rubbed during their career as a cyclist. We each find a soigneur who can tune our legs well and hope to have him work on our bodies through the season. A good soigneur can calm the rider, can give him confidence, and can heal his aches.

He strokes my legs as I speak on the phone with my wife. We chat about the day, our sons and the coming days. My voice is weak and monotone – I know this not because I am aware of it but because I have heard my team-mates speaking to their wives. The race begins to drain any energy we have for conversations. We are living in the bubble we create within the race environment and our focus becomes singular. Eat, sleep, and pedal. During the day, we walk only a few metres to save energy. Rumeau told me: "Sit instead of standing, lie flat instead of sitting." Wherever we were, at hotels or airports, he would pull up a chair for me, give me his, or find somewhere for me to sit. Rarely did we have a conversation where the two of us were standing. My legs were always to be rested for the battle on the bike.

In the soigneur's hotel room, the beds are stacked against the wall so he can unfold and set up his massage table. The carpets are dirty with dust where the beds used to sit. The bedding is worn with years of use. The room has lost any elegance it may have had when the hotel first opened its doors. The burgundy sheets make me cringe. Good and bad hotels are noted on arrival but, as we are only passing through, are rarely remembered. All I need is a good shower and a nice bed. Like the towns we race in and out of, the hotels all blur together.

The scene at the start is rarely unique. Instead, it is duplicated daily as a circus takes over the local park when it arrives in town. Like the trapeze artists in the circus we are but a part of the travelling show and our lives revolve around the insular world that is created around us.

The soigneur's strokes soothe me. On the table there is a point where my mind switches from recounting the past stage to focusing on the next effort. Perhaps the moment comes when my legs begin to recover, my body relaxes and my mind can again prepare. The massage lasts an hour. I doze in and out of sleep in the last 20 minutes. The mechanic, who shares a room with the soigneur, walks in and pulls my toe in the comforting way that a professor might wink after you've answered a question correctly. The mechanic has seen me on the road, riding and suffering. He has seen every metre of the course from the back seat of the car. He doesn't say a word to me, but the tug on my toe tells me all I need to know. He pulls off his grimy clothes. The bikes are cleaned, hung back in the truck and ready for the next stage. He stretches out on the chair for a few minutes in his underwear, flicking through the channels on the television. There is an odour of sweat, grease and liniment that now overpowers the mustiness of the hotel room. The mechanic pulls off his white underwear, flicks through the television channels one more time, and finds the highlights of the race. We all watch. The coverage ends and I turn away trying to find a comfortable spot for my head on the hard table. The mechanic is in the shower.

The team will eat together. During a tour, the race routine takes every moment of our day. At dinner, we sip half glasses of wine to celebrate the victory. The celebration is brief. The next race has already begun to engulf our thoughts. In preparation we dig into piles of pasta. Two weeks into a race, food no longer satiates: it becomes more of a necessity to survive than a pleasure as our senses become dull with over-consumption.

We won. We did the job. Around the table we all prepare to do it again.

SRM Training System - [28/7/08 09.55 - 14.05 MiBa 3.52h 2885kj 114Km 33°c, 2x40/20@450-490 w: 4x4 min@tt pace w.4min.rec b/w]

Power [watt] —   Speed [kmh] ···   Altitude [m]   Temperature [°c]   Cadence [°] —   Heartrate [bpm] +

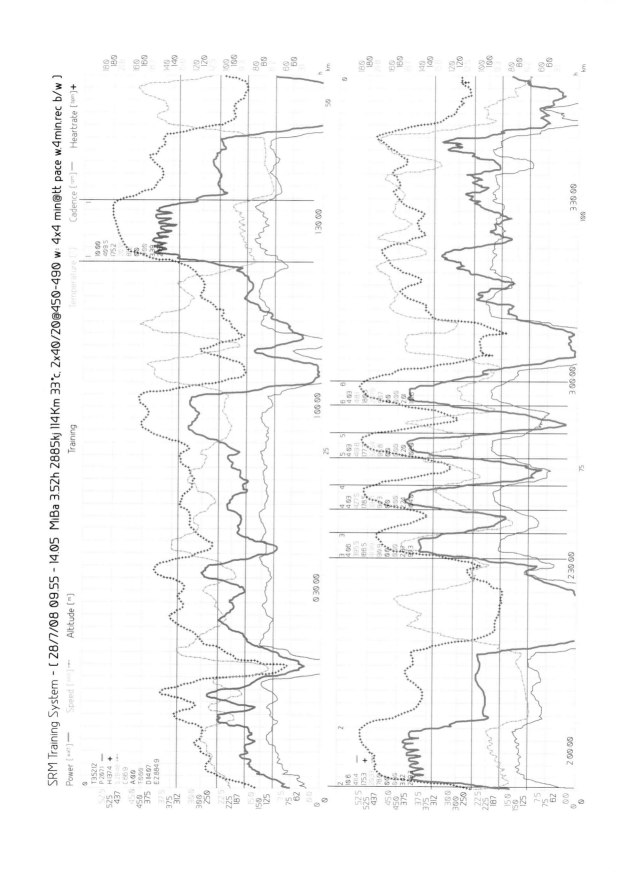

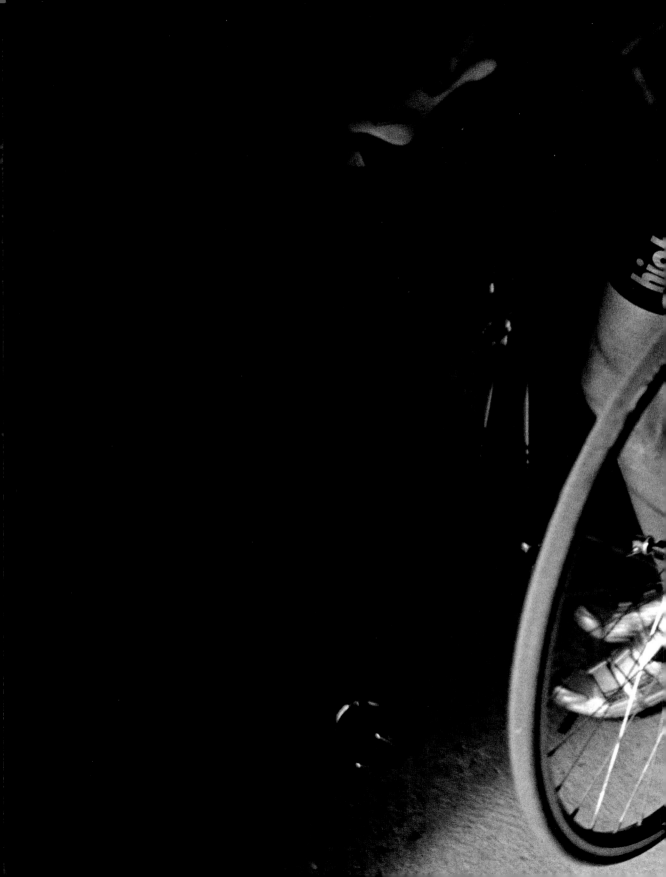

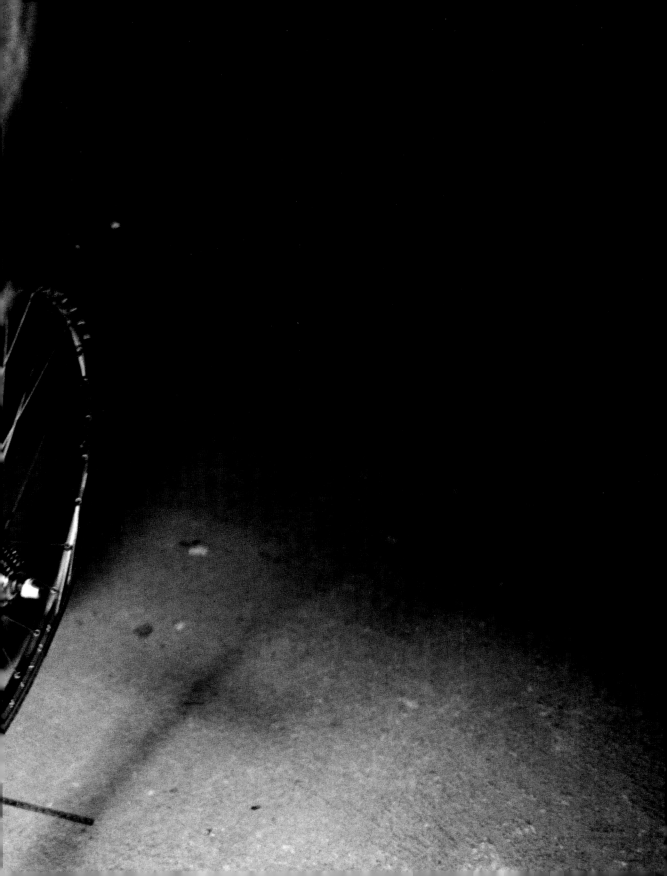

ABOVE: Café Royal, Girona.
(Barry, Millar, Hincapie, Matthew White)

OPPOSITE BELOW: La Costa del Montseny II

OPPOSITE ABOVE: At the summit of Turó de L'Home, Catalonia II

On the bus before a mountain stage. Giro d'Italia. 2009

LEFT: Col de la Croix de Fer I. Critérium du Dauphiné Libéré. 2008   RIGHT: Col de la Croix de Fer II. Critérium du Dauphiné Libéré. 2008

Col de la Croix de Fer III. Critérium du Dauphiné Libéré. 2008

AUTUMN

Into the sixth hour of the ride, the temperature drops as I reach the top of the Pyrenean peak. Autumn is arriving on the mountain slopes and the sun that burned the plains has lost its strength in the late afternoon. My shadow is long and lone on the tarmac. A ribbon of road, open and without traffic, laces its way up the treeless mountain side in front of me. A crystal mountain stream trickles. Wind blows the tall grass. Distant sounds echo in the slight wind; cattle graze on a steep slope and I occasionally hear the clangs of their bells when the breeze brushes my cheek. My breath and the ticking of my chain are the only other noises.

The mountain air is liberating after the claustrophobia of the hot valley road. Anxious truck drivers shipping goods to northern Europe and cars of tourists racing home from vacation honk with impatience. I stick to the edge of the two lane valley road counting every kilometre. Now, on the mountain, the metres pass unnoticed.

Stepping out of the saddle I re-launch my bike to maintain the fluidity I found in the first kilometres of the long ascent. I am in flight as I climb towards the sky. Settling in the saddle again, my breath is in synch with my pedal stroke and each movement is subconsciously part of the rhythm I create. I shift gears with changing gradients and readjust my position on the bike to preserve the punch of the pedal stroke.

Near the summit, the names of cyclists that were painted on the road have worn away with time. They tell the story of a race and mark a generation. Heras, Mancebo, Ullrich. Their names are fading like their results. Years ago, they stormed the climb in front of tens of thousands of fervent fans who had crossed the continent to see them ascend. Like ghosts their names now haunt cycling; they inspired with their heroics on the bike and disappointed when those performances were proven to be drug-enhanced. But their inhuman performances still endure. Stories of their elegant force are forever told.

Roberto Heras was a climber. Nicknamed 'The Cutie' by our team-mates, he was as small as a boy, with an elf-like face and a quiet demeanour. Roberto would arrive at the training camp unfit. Slowly, as the season progressed, he would become the fastest climber in the world. On a short climb at the training camp, he would be dropped by the heftiest sprinter and would struggle, holding on to the team car, to make it to the summit before the rest of the team took off down the other side. Without panic he rode himself into fitness – he knew his abilities, and he knew that with time he would reach his peak.

He was unlike any of the other leaders on the team. Hailing from a small town in central Spain, he was simple, conservative with his money, and content without the material possessions that others showed off with pride and arrogance.

A climb simplifies cycling, as the variables that make racing tactical are eliminated. Speeds are lower and drafting is no longer a great factor. The strongest riders surge ahead, paring the numbers and clarifying the tactical battle. The less the rider carries, the quicker he rides. Some look to shave off weight in everything they carry: their bodies, their shoes, their bikes and their clothing. They cut away excess material, count grams of body weight instead of kilograms, and strip their bicycles of computers and bottle cages. As overall weight decreases, watts per kilo increase along with the speed. Lean, gaunt and elf-like, a man on a bicycle can ascend like a bird in flight. Federico Bahamontes, the Spanish climbing ace of the 1950s and '60s, was nicknamed the Eagle of Toledo for his ability to soar in the mountains. Cyclists who are *en forme* can look ill when compared to an average human – we become gaunt with hollowed cheeks; our ribs protrude as muscle and fat have been stripped from our upper bodies; and flushed veins run across the skin's surface. The French say: "Un homme en forme est un homme malade." A cyclist at his peak is a sick cyclist. Not because he is unhealthy but because his body has been pushed to the limit. Like a Formula 1 car that can fly on a racetrack but can't cope with a bump in the road, our bodies are so specialised they are useless off the bike.

Heras was my room-mate at the team training camp. He was kind, thoughtful, and graceful; he asked little of others. Champion cyclists who have ascended through the ranks of society's hierarchy often develop an unpleasant arrogance due to a lack of culture and education. Like the overnight pop sensations who feed their egos on materialism and adoration, many champion cyclists fall into the trap of thinking that their careers and salaries will last eternally. Our careers are short and few make enough to retire comfortably. As their fleeting fame dissipates and their names are no longer in the papers' headlines, people who they thought were friends vanish.

Heras carried little with him. He arrived at the training camp with a virtually empty suitcase, a novel, and a suit. Jetlagged, he read for hours, sitting in the bathtub to avoid waking me and sipping on small cups on coffee in the middle of the night. At breakfast he ate halves of everything – his ritual throughout the season: half an apple with a half bowl of cornflakes.

During two Vueltas a España he was our leader. Once he finished second and once he won before he left our team. He won again while on another team and tested positive, which ended his career. *En forme* he was solitary. He rarely went to the race in the bus but opted for the team car. He had his own room in the hotel and rarely socialised with the rest of the team after meals. In the peloton we rode for him and for the objective of winning, but his victories seemed solitary – won on the tops of mountains – and they were never shared between team-mates like those of a sprinter. To us, his victories lacked emotion. To him, the results seemed expected. He won with predetermined ease.

As he soared up the climbs, we, the domestiques, struggled to make it to the finish. In the mountains, we were in a different race. We suffered to survive while he executed planned attacks. The apparent gap in ability was disturbing. He climbed with purity – a façade of purity – but there was beauty in his flight.

During his suspension, I would see him out on the Catalan roads, training alone. For him, there is no longer a finish line, but I know he persists because passion remains. The feeling of flight never leaves our memories and is one we'll eternally work to rediscover.

Alone, as I near the Pyrenean peak, I feel fast. The only person I race against is myself, and the ghosts that I create. I throttle towards the summit, accelerating hard out of the tight switchbacks and glancing at the road ahead while focusing on the peak above. The kilometre markers posted at the roadside seem to come every couple of minutes. I don't need to look at my powermeter to know I am fit. The data it stores will be all that records my effort. With nobody to judge me or compete against me, and no spectators to witness the effort, this is a solitary experience race I create. It is only the race that will invoke a rare emotion. I can see my imagined finish line at the top.

There, I will stop. I'll look down on the valley below, at the road I have just ascended, and at the peaks around me. I will sip from my bottle. I will pull on my jacket. I will be alone. A few cows will chew on grass near the roadside – they'll glance up as I near them and then bow towards the grass, continuing to eat. Beside them, a stone monument tells the story of the mountain or a saint. I will zip up my jacket, climb on my bike, and begin the long descent. I feel free but never alone.

The bike glides through the corners. I tap my brakes minimally while using my body weight to carve through the turn. Without a car in sight I use every metre of the road. Every centimetre. The switchbacks that lace up the mountain pass become a playground, like the city streets of Toronto and the thick traffic were for me as a kid. The dangers are there, but in the moment I am not conscious of them; I feel completely in control and able to find the line and the limit.

As I accelerate out of a corner and into a steep straightaway, the bike takes off. Unable to pedal fast enough, I tuck my body low on the bike and I sense the surge as it accelerates again with the decrease in drag. My eyes water beneath my glasses with the cool blast of air. My face is close to my handlebars and my chest rests on the bicycle's stem. As I near another corner I rise out of the position, which slows me like parachute does a dragster. In minutes I have descended a mountain that has taken me an hour to climb.

The maximum speed on the speedometer reads 96 km/h. The small tyres and super light carbon bike carry me comfortably – in the moment, I rarely question their strength or think of them failing, as to do so would indeed be my failure. Like a mountain climber trusts in the quality of his ropes, we become accustomed to the best equipment; the climber could never ascend a rock face to its peak without confidence in the material, as fear would consume his consciousness if he did.

As I reach the valley, the sounds of the surrounding environment return as the wind that had whistled into my ears as I descended abates. Like a child shutting down a video game and picking up a book, everything slows: my heart rate, my bike and my mind. I find another rhythm on the flat valley roads. Daydreams enter my thoughts. The thoughts jump around until they land on the World Championships, which are just over a month away. My season is almost over and my form is honed. The 80 days that I've already raced this season have given me a level of fitness and resilience unachievable in training. But the wear of the travel, the time away from home, and the pressure to perform are mentally draining.

Fallen leaves whip across the mountain road as the sun sits low on the horizon. The distance I have ridden has become incidental as I am accustomed to full days on my bike. There is an ache in my legs from the effort but the pain I felt in the spring after a long ride – the near disability of it – is absent. I have just flown up and over a mountain. I am high. But I also sense that it is time to find another routine again. My body and mind need a rest.

The time on the bike, at the races, and away from home creates a challenge for most cyclists. We become distant from our families and the routines at home are broken, quickly becoming unfamiliar as the season wears on. During the year, we spend more time with our team-mates than with our children. In the autumn, the wear of our punishing season is clear.

The autumn pelotons strike a contrast to those at the early season Classics. During the last races of the year, the fatigue of the long season is evident: teams have difficulty fielding full squads due to illness, injury and lack of motivation, and it seems many riders just go through the motions, to do their jobs and finish off the year. The riders who are motivated are those without future contracts or those who have planned their year to peak for the finale.

The cycling calendar is unbalanced as most teams start with a bang in the hopes of securing sponsors, race entries and media attention. They finish the year simply because they must. With good form and motivation, a rider and his team could perform tremendously in beautiful and prestigious races at the end of the year, if only they timed their peak fitness a little better. But in the end, cycling is a business and money is the priority.

During the second half of the season the same complacency, or weariness, is evident in the way the peloton races. In the spring, every rider is eager to be at the front, animating the race; to show his face and to achieve results. The races aren't faster than those in the late summer but there is greater depth in the peloton. In the autumn, many riders start races under their teams' orders and give in as soon as they reach the slightest difficulty, while in the spring those same riders chase back after crashing, covered in blood, because they still believe.

Lost in my daydreams I ride the final kilometres of the route without taking notice of the surroundings until I reach the outskirts of the small mountain town and see the town sign in the distance. I readjust my position for one more fight. This time I sit low, kicking back in the saddle while gripping the drops of the handlebars tightly. Again, I create my own race. A car passes. As if the sign were my finish line, I step out of the saddle, gauging my effort on the distance to the sign, and launch myself into a sprint, hammering the pedals. The bike thrashes from side to side beneath me. The effort is fierce. I imagine a competitor on my right and re-accelerate, surging, thrusting, and driving my body and the bike. I give out, I give in, as I reach the imaginary line at the town sign.

Days later, I am in an airport on my way to the final stage race of the season. Panicked travellers rush, sweat, curse and fret around me. Comfortable in the routine I wait, find my place, listen to music, and watch the shuffle of bags, the bumps of bodies, and the flash of faces as they pass through the terminal in haste. Planes roar away while others roll up. The excitement of travel has become mundane with repetition.

At the other end, in another terminal in another country, a soigneur patiently waits for me to arrive. He has driven for an hour from the hotel to be my chauffeur. During the drive we gossip about cycling – which riders are transferring to which teams, the results, the races, the difficulties and complaints. Within our bubble, we lose perspective: small abnormalities and complaints become amplified as they circulate, turning into an irritant. The soigneurs, like the mechanics, seem to be informed on everything within the team like a secretary who oversees an office.

Arriving at the hotel, the mechanics are working on the bikes under the spotlights of the team truck. The air compressor hums behind the din of electronic music. Dressed in blue work clothes, their hands covered in grease, they bop to the music as they shift through gears, pump tyres, and screw on number plates. Three other team trucks are lined up beside them with mechanics at work.

Like the soigneurs, they know the importance of the race because many were professional cyclists, or amateurs, or simply keen fans. Cycling is still a foreign novelty to North Americans, but to Europeans it is part of their culture. The staff take pride in their work because, on some level, they believe and understand that they are not only working on bikes; they are also a part of something greater – cultural history. That understanding, along with their work ethic and their discipline, turns their work from job to trade – they're experts in the same way that a carpenter can manipulate wood to make something that is both beautiful and reliable. They work with passion.

From the seat of the team car I can see one of the mechanics, Chris, working on my bike. Bundled up in a heavy jacket and hat, he looks up from the task and smiles as we park. During the race I will trust his work and never question it. And he will sit confidently in the car behind, knowing that nothing will fail. He will recheck my bike one last time in the morning before the start. The details make the difference.

Every evening during the race he will check the tubular rubber for cuts and wear, and a worn tubular will be replaced. Each tyre has been aged in a cellar – like a good wine they will, over time, reach their maturity where they become something unique with subtle differences in performance that a professional can feel. For each of his Tour de France victories, Armstrong rode special aged tyres that no other riders on the team had. He rarely flatted and had few difficulties over the tens of thousands of kilometres raced.

My race bike is ready. It shines like a new bike from a shop. The transition from my training bike to a race bike is like chopping tomatoes with a worn kitchen knife and then switching to a high carbon steel chef's blade. The tubular tyres glide and grip, the race wheels are stiff and smooth, and the bike is clean and crisp. Not only technically better, a race bike with aerodynamic light wheels also gives a psychological lift.

As I chat with the mechanic and as the soigneur wheels my suitcase to the hotel lobby, a team-mate rides up, having just finished a short spin. We shake hands and chat briefly. Eight months into the season he is lean and thin. His skin is dark from the hours in the sun. When I see photos of myself, I realise I look the same. Like circus trapeze artists, cyclists contrast with the crowds who come to watch the spectacle. Our identity is clear even when we wear civilian clothes: the kilometres have moulded our bodies while the climate has stained them.

Our hotel rooms have been prepared by the soigneurs; my suitcase is lined up against the wall and bottled water sits on the bedside table beside a room list that breaks down where everybody from the team is staying. A few minutes after I arrive, the soigneur will fetch me for a massage. In his room, my team-mates will gather to snack on the cookies, cereal, and fruit he has brought up for us. On the hardest race days, they'll prepare hot food to satiate our appetites and lift our morale. In a weakened state from the stress of the race, three things overwhelm every cyclist's psyche to the point of obsession: food, sleep and the bike.

The peloton is now divided between those worn by a tough spring and a hard Tour de France and those rested from a calm summer at home without racing. With enough fitness and motivation there are still some beautiful targets to aim for: the World Championships and the numerous one day autumn Classics. But when a rider is tired, each day is counted until the end of the year. His pedal stroke will be laboured and he will remain tight in the draft of the peloton until he is eventually dropped.

Like students talking about their summer plans, riders on the team gossip about who has re-signed, who will leave and where they will go. Some riders are relaxed as they have signed their contracts and have achieved the needed results. They feel that they can freewheel through the rest of the season while others, nervous they may not find the contract they desire, panic like juniors as they fight to achieve what they weren't able to earlier in the year.

The riders who finished the Tour de France a month ago share stories while team-mates smile, not exactly able to comprehend the story, as the bond built between the Tour team-mates separate them from the rest. They speak about how their bodies have recovered, what they did to celebrate their arrival in Paris, and where they will be off to next.

In the peloton, some of the Tour riders pedal confidently, spinning their legs with ease, while others, knowing they are riding one of their last races of the year, forecast their ambition of riding to satisfy the team – they are planning on retiring from the race before the end of the week. I know that on the bike those who are motivated will be strong and confident having completed the Tour without injury or illness. A three week Grand Tour changes a rider in a way no other effort can, but with a week of rest the body rebounds. There is a perception built around the comfort of good fitness, that the climbs are shallower and shorter and the races slightly slower. Three relentless weeks of racing gives a rider a level of strength unobtainable in training.

A week into the short stage race, it is clear that the team is committed to the victory and to each other. Our pre-racing meetings are brief and succinct. We know our jobs, our roles, our fitness, and the course – the directeur simply reiterates the essentials like a professor might before his students sit an exam.

In the team bus, I am comfortable in the rhythm I have found during the year, travelling from finish to hotel and then from hotel to start with my team-mates. We chat, we sleep, we eat, and we live together. It is a routine I have enjoyed – we accept the idiosyncrasies of others while discovering a certain level of comfort in the habitual life. In the bus, we each find our comfortable spot, creating a den. In the mornings, the coffee machine spits out espressos and after the race we crush empty plastic bottles as we try to rehydrate. The peculiarities of a shared life, which used to be funny, become irritating now in the same way a classroom of kids becomes obnoxious on a Friday afternoon. The pungent odour of leg balms, the stale stink that wafts from the bathroom, and the chatter of the team getting ready to race or winding down the day can become tiresome when you are thinking of a family at home.

We leave the bus at intervals with exits based on personal motivations. Some riders depart early as they're eager to chat to friends and family, while others linger until the final moment to relax in the isolated comfort of the bus. We sign in to the race on a podium and the announcer blasts our names and past results to the crowd. We could be in any town. The race is our focus and it has replaced the normality of the small town life with marching bands, loudspeakers, brightly coloured banners and a motorcade of buses, trucks, campers, and cars. The towns we see all look similar when the circus we animate wraps them in a fresh façade for a few hours.

As we roll out of town, the race neutralised until we reach the city limit, I can sense nervousness in the peloton. The chatter of a flat formulaic stage is absent as everybody knows the race for the overall classification could swing. We are eager to attack. Our rivals are focused on the defence and not the stage victory. Some simply fear the difficulties ahead – each rider faces his own battle no matter what thoughts lie heavy on his mind. Some riders are already defeated and their only concern is making it to the finish.

With the drop of the commissaire's neutral flag, the race starts with vigour. Riders attack; others chase. No attack lasts longer than a minute as the riders relent as soon as they realise the peloton is pursuing and the gap hasn't formed. As the attacker sits up, another rider pops out of the draft of the peloton and attempts to do what the last has failed to accomplish. The speed of the peloton remains high, as the pursuit is constant despite the staccato tempo at the front imposed by the attacks.

In time, the pace, the accelerations and the undulating terrain begin to wear the group out. Riders yell that we should stop for a pee, as they need a rest. Sensing their fatigue, we continue to attack and the group begins to break

OBAIN SAINT-GOBAIN

202

into fragments. Like water beads joining to form a larger pool, the riders slowly accumulate behind the front group. Some chase in panic, hoping to regain contact, while others resign, relent on the pedals, and settle into a steady speed that will get them to the line within the time cut. Up front, we know that the dropped are no longer a factor.

The peloton, once plump with 140 strong riders, has withered to about 20 under the pressure of the race. Only a few of those are a threat as the rest are struggling to follow. The continuously undulating climbs over the 180 kilometre course have worn the group as we have attacked each short climb with a potent burst over the summit. The race could swing either way. Tired, riders begin to ride in desperation to protect their position in the classification. With little to lose and everything to gain our team continues to attack with the goal of making the race ours.

And the barrage of attacks never relents. The leading team sets a tempo to chase on the front. Their team splinters and then regroups with each climb and each burst from the peloton. As the race wears on, fewer of their number return and then, their leader is isolated. This is the moment we have fought for; we are in a position to profit.

As the group of 20 surges and slows, riders are dropped and have to fight to regain contact. Their grimaces of pain tell me my legs are better than anybody's in the group. With each surge I feel better, knowing their tolerance is abating. My potency augments as I gain confidence. The large gear that I'm riding carries the bike fluidly. *En forme*. The bike moves quickly up the climbs and flies over their summits. Like a knockout boxer in the ring, I look to my rivals when they attack wondering if that is the best they've got. On the start line, I didn't know how my body would handle the course, but after pedalling through the first kilometres I know I have the legs to win. As the race nears its end, that sensation only grows.

Following a rival's burst from the group, I sink low on my bike, sitting tight in his draft. I have followed dozens of similar attacks since the start of the stage, but this one is timed right as our group has relaxed, having just charged after a similar surge. My rival has picked the right moment to attack and knowing from experience that this move will be decisive, I follow.

There are thousands of moments within a race that could potentially decide the outcome, but the experienced rider can pick the exact moment, like a gambler who has studied the odds and knows the competition. *En forme*, the moment I would attack becomes clear as I can see the race with lucidity. Panic, stress and pain will blur focus. A baseball player who is in the zone can see the seams of the ball as it hurtles toward him. He can almost see the ball as it come into contact with his bat. Free of panic, he can concentrate. I know that the riders who are behind can no longer comprehend the tactics of the race; they are fighting with every watt they can produce just to stay in contact with the group. Their focus has gone from winning to surviving.

On the wheel, tight in the draft, my legs spin my smallest cog at over 100 revolutions per minute. I glance behind me. There are two riders in my slipstream and, even though the attack has only lasted ten seconds, there is already a significant gap between the four of us and the group behind. The group is still a small bubble in the road as their pursuit, which will drive them into a single line, has not yet begun. They will hold off chasing for a few more minutes as most of the riders have given in and look to each other to close the gap; they are thinking of the finish, their wasted legs, and maintaining what they have already achieved. They are no longer willing to sacrifice everything for the victory, but they are willing to ride for the places of honour, hoping to maintain their positions in the overall race classification.

Seeing the gap, and sensing the slowing tempo of the rider in front, I accelerate in a burst of power I know I can sustain for over a minute. The rider who I was following tucks into my slipstream while only one of the others can follow us. One is dropped. I look back at his grimacing face as he fights with his body to push it beyond the level it can go. There is desperation in his face. If he doesn't close the gap immediately, he knows that he has no chance of catching us again – he'll flounder in between groups before eventually resigning himself to his destiny and being absorbed into the draft of the peloton. Knowing this, I push a little harder on the pedals and he's gone. Now we are three.

We take equal turns on the front, each pedalling hard enough to forge the gap between the groups. The goal is to be out of sight and to gain enough time – two minutes or more – that we can comfortably race towards the finish without fear of the group behind catching us. Each of us takes the occasional glance behind to gauge the gap, and then yells a few short words of encouragement to keep the trio moving. If each rider's effort is equal in duration and speed, we will succeed. From my odometer, I can tell there are just over 20 kilometres until the finish. We'll pass the sign marking the distance in a few minutes. From then on, there will be a sign every five kilometres until the last kilometre. Then it is the metres that are counted.

In the final burst to the line, every pedal stroke hurts as the build-up of lactic acid reaches a peak. For the fans, it is in those metres that they crane over the barriers to see the faces, the movements, and feel the speed of the riders as a five hour race culminates in 20 seconds of action.

Over the race radio my directeur begins to give me instructions and information. He tells me what the time gap is, who is chasing behind, which riders from our team are in the chase group, and where our virtual times stack up in the general classification. I listen to bits and pieces, selecting the important information by distinguishing it from emotion.

I want a solo victory.

My companions in the breakaway are fatiguing rapidly. Their efforts in the lead position are becoming slower and shorter, and I can sense their misery with each rotation of our group. They're losing morale and simply want the race to be over. They have reached the point of transition where they are no longer thinking of winning, but of making it to the finish and maintaining everything they have already fought hard for.

On a long shallow gradient, I push a little harder as I tow the train. My powermeter reads over 500 watts. "Fuck, slow down! Steady!" yells one of my companions. Knowing they're struggling, I accelerate harder. My powermeter reads over 600 watts. I look back: we are three and there are 15 kilometres to go. My legs feel better with each surge. My confidence grows as theirs dies. Over the radio I can hear the excitement of the directeur. He encourages me. "You're not going to get caught now. It is sure. The gap is too large. You can win this."

Since turning professional my victories have been few. As a boy, a teenager and an amateur, I won often. Those triumphs came easily; I worked for them, I fought for them, but the competition was never as fierce or as desperate as with my professional rivals. The moment is rare when I am flying and the race plays out tactically in my favour. I realise my weaknesses, accept them and work to overcome them. It is my innately competitive spirit that pushes me to battle until the end, forcing me to believe that eventually the victory will come. And it does – just not as often as it once did.

As we enter the finishing circuit in the centre of the small town, I sense that my companions are struggling. They are asking for mercy. I accelerate out of a corner on a rising road and they are gone. I am alone and there are ten kilometres to go.

In those ten kilometres, my thoughts switch. The tactical game is over. The finish is my focus: I accelerate out of the corners, pedal at a high cadence on the descents, and power up the short climbs to maintain a consistently high speed.

A motorbike revs around me. Noticing the camera I think about my family watching the race live on television at home – and my son who always asks if I won when I return home from a race. To him, the whole point is the victory. He is too young to see the difficulties, the sacrifice, and to understand my passion. The essence is winning, but the journey is what makes that moment sublime. In 20 years I have learned much; I now enjoy what I do more profoundly. A painter can paint to sell or he can paint his emotions and thoughts; money and fame are fleeting while enlightened pieces painted with affection will inspire.

I know that the memories of my few moments receiving accolades will soon fade, but I also know that the feeling I had when I executed the decisive attack will remain. I know that in bed, I will feel elated as I look up at the ceiling and look back on the ride. It is the same emotion after a long day of training or a race day. The victory is fleeting while the effort is eternal.

Coming out of the final corner, there is one short climb and then a flat bit before the finish line. It will take me roughly 40 seconds to cover the distance. I know I have won. I can't feel my legs; there is no pain any more. I grip my bars tightly as I accelerate up the climb. Out of the saddle, my bike sways like a pendulum with each pedal stroke. Riding into the tunnel of cheers created by the crowds who are held back by the barriers that funnel me towards the finish, I hear the announcer belting out my name with a thunderous voice intended to animate the crowd. With 200 metres to go I ease off the pedals, sit up, letting my handlebars go and my body extend towards the sky.

As I coast the last few metres over the line, I take no notice of the spectators around me. I look for our soigneur who will give me a bottle and wipe my face. I need a moment alone with my thoughts and a drink. The only people with whom I wish to share the moment are my family because only they might understand. The water goes down smoothly. I calm myself, putting my head on my handlebars for a few seconds, and take a deep breath. My hands shake slightly. Muscles twitch. I look up to a throng of surging reporters who thrust microphones and hurl questions. Resting on my bike, I listen, chat, and smile. The job continues.

The podium is a formality through which we are hustled as the live television has a schedule to follow. Kisses, handshakes, smiles and flowers. Since I crossed the line a chaperone has watched me closely. He will stay at my side, eyeing every movement and everything I ingest until I finally reach the doping control. After the ceremony, the day's leaders and winner are then ushered to the press conference.

In the makeshift set-up in the local high school gym, we sit behind three long tables with microphones on their tops. Before the official conference begins, we sip on drinks and chat about the race like students gossiping about their class-mates and what has just happened over the lunch break. Like parents trying to grasp what their children are doing all day at school, few of the media understand our chatter. Once we are introduced and the media fire off their questions, scribbling notes, our faces change, as we all know the answers need to represent our own, our sponsors', and the sport's best interests. Adolescents tell their parents the story they want to hear to satisfy them – and many of the answers we reel off are similar to those we have been taught in media training.

The race takes place in a complicated world of relationships, tactics and rivalries. When presented to the public, that realm is often less colourful as it is dulled to please. Few people who aren't riders or staff are ever fully immersed in the environment, which creates a tightly insular world. The shared experiences transcend our lives outside this confined environment; few can properly explain the emotional relationship and experiences that develop between the riders.

As we work through the questions, there is a formality to the session that nobody really seems to enjoy. We, the cyclists, only want to get to the hotel for a shower and some food, while the media are rushing to meet their deadlines. We are still at work. The true stories from the race will be told at dinner between the boys on the team.

An announcer pushes us through the questions and then out the door toward the doping control caravan.

Medical testing is a part of my life that has become routine – like paying taxes, it is something I understand is a necessity but not something I enjoy.

Since my first year on the national team, as a 15-year-old, I have been tested. The first tests were almost a novelty that somehow gave me a feeling of accomplishment: I was good enough to be tested.

The small caravan is parked in the middle of the now empty high school parking lot with a makeshift sign posted on the door designating its purpose: 'Doping Control'. Near the caravan, a crew of workmen tears down the stands, loads the metal crowd-retaining barricades onto trucks, and packs up the finish line. The spectators have now dispersed aside from the few diehard fans who wait outside the doping caravan for an autograph and a photo. I was once one of them.

Entering the caravan I know the routine that is to follow. I rip open sealed bags, fill plastic jars with my urine, and fill out forms. Dehydrated, my urine is mustard yellow, and I push out just enough to fill the pot to the required threshold. Some riders, unable to produce enough urine, must wait patiently and drink. Only when I am tested at home, in front of my children, do I feel that my privacy is being invaded – the testing process is a difficult one to explain to young children, especially when the doorbell rings before dawn and my blood is taken. Once the bags are sealed and the papers signed, I am free. The workday is over.

The drive to the hotel from the race is one I have always enjoyed. As an amateur, on the long car journeys home from the race, Rumeau and I would chat about the day as I munched on spice cake, sipped on cola, and ate my ham sandwich. The radio hummed in the background. The car had the aroma of the race: grease, fresh air and clean sweat. As his apprentice, I absorbed everything Rumeau told me, hoping only to improve: cycling is Rumeau's life, and I didn't want to let him down. As a mentor, he pushed me and carried my performance. He still does. As I have matured, certain individuals have become a part of me through their guidance and advice. Even though oceans separate us, or heavens, I still feel an obligation to them to produce the best I can. Respect for them makes me fear their disappointment.

Returning to the hotel, I pass through my team-mates' rooms to thank them for their help before stripping down and entering the shower. The congratulations are sincere and their embraces warm. Their faces are alight as they talk about their race in the peloton that pursued me. I snack on a few cookies and sip on water as we chat. My body continues to race. Sitting down I can feel my heart pumping rapidly as sweat beads drop from my forehead. When we push our bodies beyond the normal limits, they will work to recover for hours after the stress has abated – the next stage is still hours away.

As the warm shower water cascades over my body, cleaning off a layer of sweat, dirt and spit, I feel accomplished. The shower is one of the few moments in the day when I am alone. I have danced in the shower after a race. And, when the sacrifice has been so great and the goal has not been achieved, I have cried. On a team, we live together but we each deal with the difficulties alone. On a bike, the challenge is more personal than competitive.

To prepare us for the 1996 Olympics in Atlanta, the Canadian national team rode together in a German stage race one month prior to the Games. Steve Bauer was my room-mate and team-mate. During that event, my childhood hero not only became a friend but also advised me like a coach, in a way that has had an impact on my career. In the race he was calm, could tell us when to be up front in the wind or when to sit behind in the wheels, when to attack and when doing so was futile; he could see the pattern of the race, how the peloton would attack the course, and who would be there in the finale. He had worn the Tour de France yellow jersey, had been on the podium in Roubaix, and had animated the finales of the finest races. That experience had developed an innate knowledge and confidence. Not only did he know the races, but he also knew his body and when it was ready to win.

During the race through the hilly Rhineland, we shared a hotel room. Every night we would chat with the lights out about the day and the coming stage before he finally said: "Okay, better get to sleep. Sleep good."

Steve hadn't performed well during the first days of the two week race. He struggled in the hills and didn't seem to have the fight or flight of a winner. The night of the second to last stage, just before he said, "Sleep good," he asked: "Do you think I can win tomorrow?" I responded: "Sure, why not?"

"I will. Sleep good."

I closed my eyes wondering if it was confidence, arrogance, or knowledge. The race had been hard as there was an elite peloton of riders all refining their fitness before the Olympics – it was a race where dozens of riders had the power to win and dozens more were eager to try. To predict a victory seemed brash.

In the last 20 kilometres, Steve attacked alone at the top of the final ascent. He held off the charging peloton and won by a slim few seconds. I was impressed. That night, just before falling asleep, he asked me the same question: "Do you think I can win again?"

The following day he won in similar fashion, with panache. He knew his body, knew the peloton, understood the tactics, and feared nobody. He was *en forme*.

Over a decade later I have slowly developed a sense of my body from experiences. As a boy I rode hard whenever there was a finish line. My efforts were never planned or gauged; I couldn't sense the subtleties of being fit and wasn't aware of the rhythmic fluidity I produced when I was flying. I simply went at it like a teenager puts his foot to the floor of his new hotrod to show off the power it can produce, with complete disregard for how the car actually handles and performs under pressure. I would only discover that I was tired when my engine was blown because I was sick or had lost all motivation to ride. Through trial and error – and through listening to Rumeau, Steve, and my coaches – I began to pay attention to how well my body was moving on the bike and when to step on it or when to ease off on the throttle. The body cannot go full speed for a whole season: as veterans we learn to push when we have it, and build or rebuild when we don't.

Each cyclist fights an internal battle. Some fight on the bike because it gives them purpose and simplifies the complexities in life. Others escape. Others ride to fill a void. Others battle childhood disturbances. Others pedal for fitness or weight loss. We each have our reasons.

The race grime cleaned off, I pull on my team tracksuit. A soigneur taps on the slightly open door and asks if I am ready for a massage. I follow him down the hallway of the dingy hotel to his room. The beds have been pushed aside to allow enough room for the massage table. The white sheets look clinical against the maroon carpet and floral bedding. I pull off my pants, climb on the bed and settle. I close my eyes. My leg muscles twitch from the effort. My thoughts rewind and fast forward, to my past and to tomorrow. I feel high.

Over the hundreds of thousands of kilometres I've ridden, I've slowly come to realise why my desire developed and became an obsession. Without it, I struggle – I am anxious, unfocused and tense. Cycling has become spiritual, as it is a passion that I can pursue in the natural environment. I can pedal away angst, find calm and clarity with the rhythmic motion and freedom. The commitment gives me a focus; the love gives me panache. Whether it is pedalling to a victory or training in the mountains, I find peace.

SRM Training System - [28/09/08 10:12 - 17:16 MiBa 6.1h 5736kj 214Km 22°c. World Championships Varese. / lap 3/crash, rode with spare bike.]

Power [watt] — Speed [km/h] — Temperature [°] — Cadence [rpm] — Heartrate [bpm] +

Training Altitude [m]

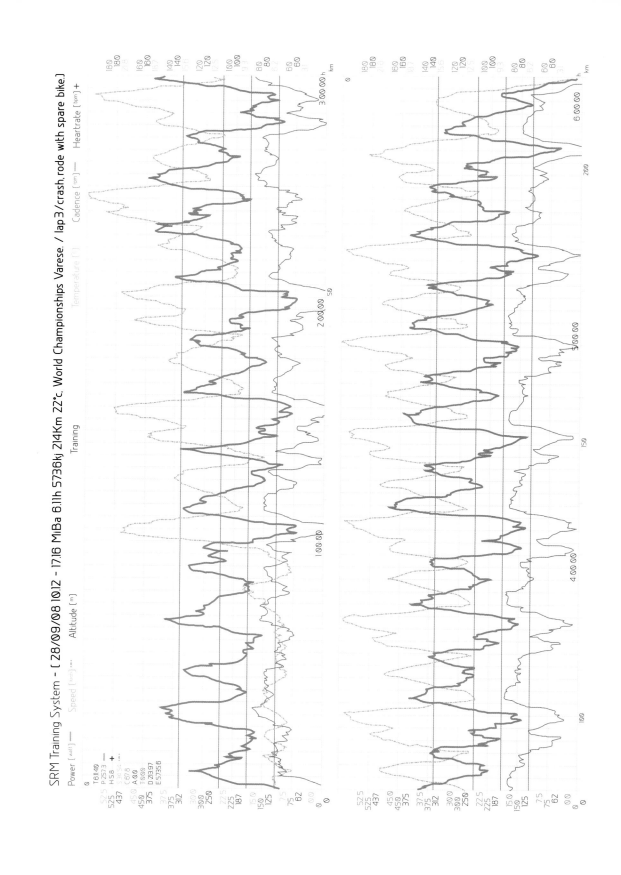

PREVIOUS IMAGE: Full gas through the Ozark. Tour of Missouri. 2008

Michael cruising in the paceline. Tour of Missouri. 2008

RIGHT: With the directeur sportif in St Louis II. Tour of Missouri. 2008

LEFT: With the directeur sportif in St Louis I. Tour of Missouri. 2008

Michael takes the stage and the most aggressive rider's jersey, Stage 4, Tour of Missouri, 2008 ‖ PREVIOUS PAGE: 20km to go on the Mississippi Delta Tour of Missouri, 2008

BOTTOM LEFT: Backstage in Rolla. Michael will get this most aggressive rider's jersey   TOP LEFT: The press in Rolla I

RIGHT: Staying in a hotel on Alfreda Binda Plaza and passing the U23 world champion's room

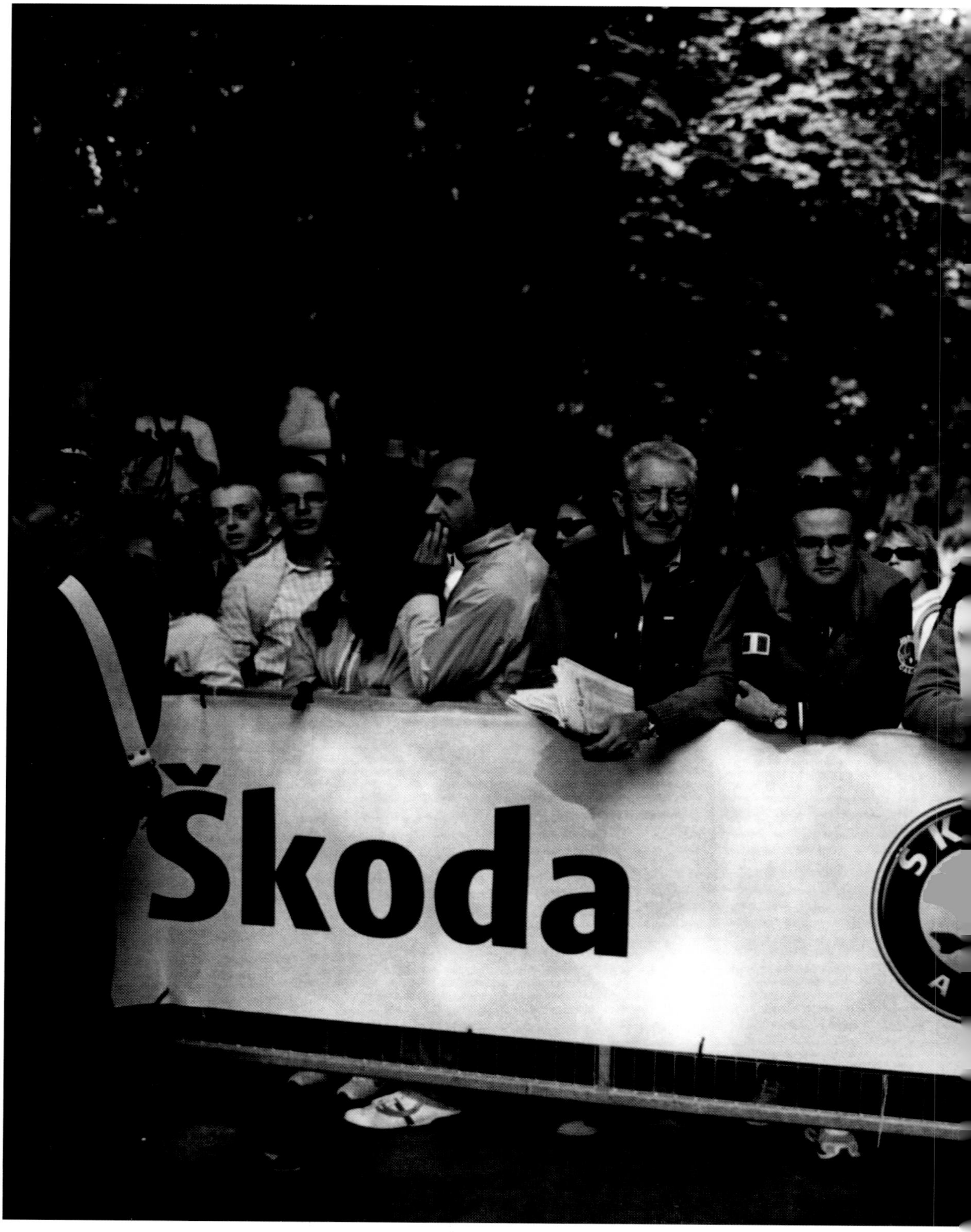
Škoda

Tifosi before the start of the Men's Road Racing Championship, Varese, 2008

TOP RIGHT: Varese III, 2008

BOTTOM RIGHT: A finished rider has his tag unceremoniously taken off

TOP LEFT: Varese I, 2008

BOTTOM LEFT: Varese II, 2008

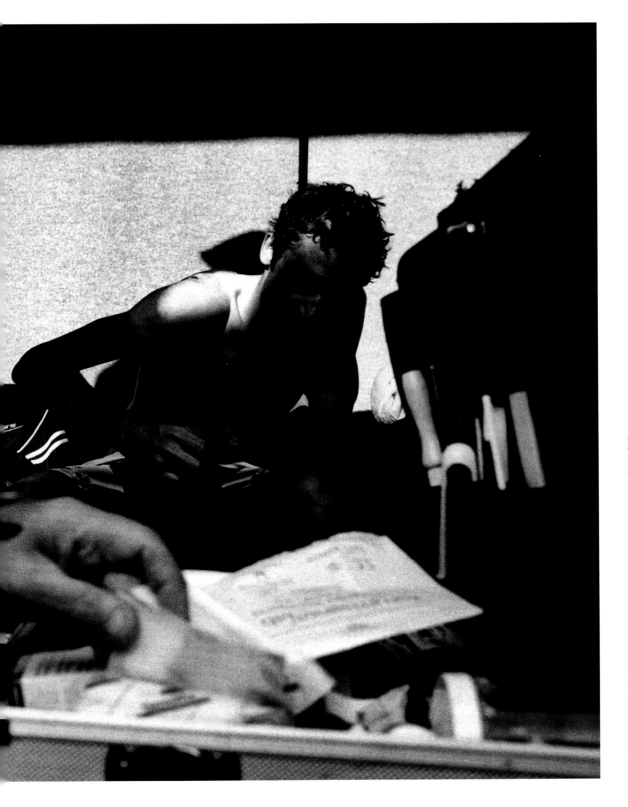

Pantà de Susqueda, Catalonia

Cavendish talks to his girlfriend after another stage win at the Tour of Missouri. 2008

AFTERWORD

The air conditioning and humidifier made the air heavy. A shaft of light pierced the darkness of the room. The dent in my pillow was damp with sweat. I turned away from the light and into the darkness of the unfamiliar room to find a few more minutes of rest. Closing my eyes again I quickly realised the anticipation of the day would overwhelm any hope of sleep. I had waited for this day forever.

Turning back into the light, I played the day's race out in my head as my eyes fixed on the beam of light which cut the room in two. In training I had ridden the short prologue course repeatedly and knew every metre well enough to envision it. Yet from experience I also knew that the spectators, the barriers, the banners, the weather and the emotion of the race would transform the course into something almost unrecognisable. The mental images had my heart racing. Despite having raced thousands of events over decades, moments remain when I still feel a boy's nervous anticipation: the night before Paris-Roubaix, the World Championships, the Olympics and the Giro. My emotions now eclipsed everything I had felt before. I was about to roll down the start ramp at the Tour de France.

Ten days before the Grand Départ in Rotterdam, my phone rang. After a hard day of training I sat in the passenger seat as my wife drove our loaded car to the coast. Worn out by the Spanish heat, our boys dozed in the back seat. The phone call was one I was anxiously anticipating. As in the previous seven years, this call would determine not only how I spent July but whether or not

I would achieve a lifelong goal as well. Years of disappointment had prepared me for the worst. Instinct told me that my dream would be fulfiled. A few words into the conversation I knew I was going. A hundred or so other riders had similar conversations with their directeurs throughout June. Some were left devastated, others elated. The Tour transcends everything.

At the age of eight, I toured France with my father on a tandem. It was my first introduction to Europe, the mountains and everything I had read about and gazed at in Vélo Mag and Miroir du Cyclisme. Over two weeks, we rode from Grenoble to Marseilles, up Mont Ventoux, and over roads marked by the Tour's passing. For me France has always been cycling. I phoned my parents as soon as I found out that I had been selected. Tears rolled down my cheek and my voice shuddered when they answered. Since I was a boy they had supported my persistence and my commitment to racing.

The next person I phoned was the directeur of my amateur team in France, Christian Rumeau. The Tour route included the Haute-Savoie region and specifically Annemasse, the town where I had lived for several years and apprenticed before becoming a professional. After a decade of discussing the possibility of my entering the Tour, Rumeau would now be there along the roadside. Before hanging up, he advised me on how to ride the pavé on the stage into the town of Arenberg, how to approach the first week and what my role should be within the team. I absorbed it but didn't realise how right he was until the race had ended. He hadn't lost his nose for bike racing.

Nervously, I approached the start ramp. Prologues and time trials are a routine part of racing. But the weight of the lenses and watching eyes gave this one an uncomfortable gravity. The start house resembles a blow-up jungle gym painted with logos. As I stepped inside, I felt alone in a tunnel. The faces surrounding me blurred as I focused on the race. The clock ticked away the seconds until my departure. I remained in the tunnel after I launched down the road. The barriers, spectators, flags and noise enveloped the course. After a deep breath, I felt the tug of my tight skinsuit against my expanding lungs. The intake of air slowed everything down. Nervousness became clarity during the moment when I saw the police motorcycle ahead, under an inflatable Tour de France banner. Emotion took hold, my eyes welled with tears and I smiled. A career of cycling, a childhood dream shared with my parents, culminated in that moment. Another deep breath. A tug of fabric. This is it. Let's get on with it. Enjoy it and do my best.

With the race underway, everything fell into the routine which has become my life as a professional cyclist. Within our insular environment the Tour is similar to any other major race. But the crowds, the attention and the stakes are greater. That fills the peloton with an agitated nervousness. Due to the magnitude of the event, we lose perspective. Panic is amplified during the first week. Riders who will be hours behind the leaders at the finish in Paris fight for seconds. The hierarchy has yet to be established and everybody is eager to leave his mark on the Tour. But the race will humble most riders, as inevitably it will strip away façades to show weakness.

Through the chaotic first week crashes were numerous. Few riders weren't bandaged, bruised or limping. The cyclists' battle is constant. With hope, we learn to suppress pain in order to race another day. Only when the finish line is crossed do our minds allow our bodies to relax. In the Tour that moment doesn't come until Paris. Cyclists are optimists. Injured, we ride in pouring rain for hundreds of kilometres over mountains, hoping, praying and knowing it will eventually relent. The race is our job. We persist and resist because there is a team, a nation of fans, desire and commitment.

Through the Tour, my job was to ride alongside our leader, Bradley Wiggins, and keep him protected from the wind, in position and well fuelled. It was a job I had done before in other races and one which I find gratifying. The goal was to help him place in the top three in the general classification. Cyclists sacrifice for months, or more, to arrive at the start of the Tour de France *en forme*. Like a top student studying for his finals, Bradley had done his work with precision. But he struggled in the toughest moments. The *coup de pédale*, which had carried him to fourth in an earlier Tour and numerous Olympic medals, was absent.

In cycling there are dozens of variables which can't be tested or tried because they're innate. Bradley had sacrificed and suffered. But perhaps it had all been too calculated and he hadn't followed instinct built on experience. The team did its job. Bradley rode to his limits. Fitness can be elusive. You think you have it and then it disappears. You think you're dead and you're flying. You win and then crash.

As we neared Annemasse at the end of the first week, I was without the potency I had felt while training on the same roads two weeks before the start. A crash had taken it out of me. We continue without complaint yet that doesn't mean every movement isn't painful. We focus on the future with hope. That hope helps us overcome. The gravity of the injury was secondary to the importance of the race. While climbing, each pain is accentuated as everything slows; muscles are strained and sweat no longer evaporates before it burns wounds. But I was on roads I knew well. Rumeau would be at the hotel. My parents would be at the finish. I had a job to do.

The searing heat through the first week of the Tour wilted the peloton, sapping the will to animate the race from each day's start. It left us ragged. Through the Alps riders fell repeatedly simply from fatigue. Yet these familiar roads brought me some comfort. As an amateur 14 years ago I rode them almost daily. Back then, I imagined that I was in the Tour de France, sparring with the best while racing over the iconic climbs I had read about as a boy. But it wasn't only the roads that made me feel at ease. It was also the familiarity of the shops, the café where I had stopped with team-mates, the farmhouse painted with a Dubonnet advertisement. The countryside and the town were laced with memories which suddenly put my life in place as I was living a moment I had imagined. Sacrifice and patience had brought depth to my life.

Rumeau came to the hotel and we chatted as if not a day had passed since I was 20; as if he was again back at my apartment in Annemasse sitting at the dining room table advising me like a father his boy. Comforting friendship brought hope, which eclipsed the pain.

Towns, climbs, and stages all become a blur as we become captivated by the Tour. We focus on the wheel in front, the road ahead, the distance markers, and only capture glimpses of the environment in a whirl of speed. The moments that become memories are never predictable. Those moments enriched my life in a way I hadn't imagined as they coloured the story I had dreamed since I was a boy.

With the Seine on our right and the city surrounding us, the speed lifted as if a conductor had just directed a symphony to increase tempo. Minutes later our radios crackled with spoken orders. The job. The team found each other as we sped under bridges and riders threw bidons to lighten their load before the finale. The peloton began to race with the chaotic fury to which we had become accustomed. As I raced to the front of the group, the Eiffel Tower became apparent in the distance. In a swell of emotion, my eyes blurred with tears, I thought of my wife and boys, my father and mother at the finish, the trip to France on the tandem. In a few seconds there was a culmination of everything that had passed. And then, the finish line.

Sky bus – tactical meeting the night before. 2010

EPILOGUE

Lying on the massage table, I stare at the ceiling tinged yellow with age and smoke. Before and after races, I gaze blankly at walls, ceilings and television screens as I either prepare for the race or reflect on it. This evening I replay the race in my thoughts. The first attack I was able to follow. The second was too much. So I waited. The fourth I followed, but by then it was too late. A moment's hesitation had cost me. Now I was attempting to grapple with the consequences. Being close but not close enough during the decisive moment leaves a racer filled with regrets that last through the night. If those regrets aren't wiped clean by another performance, they become eternal. Close is never enough.

The soigneur pushes deep into my quadriceps, digging at the knots in the muscles. The fierce effort, up and over the last climb, did the damage he's working to repair. In the final 100 metres of the short sharp climb, I fought to close a small gap. The riders I needed to reach were dangling only metres in front of me. Their slipstream would have been a lifeline: allowing me to ease off the pedals for a few seconds, recovering just enough to push again. But my legs gave out before I could reach it. Four riders rode away and I was left alone, fighting a losing battle with the wind, my mind, my legs and my rivals. Aware that a lone chase was futile, I waited for others. But when they arrived I realised their legs were too weak to help. On the massage table, I look for answers in the plaster ceiling. The races remain with us.

Closing my eyes, I can still feel the pedal strokes and hear the fans' cheers. Their expressions had been a blur while I focused on the riders ahead. Retrospect kills the pain felt during the race. We deceive ourselves into believing the effort was less than fierce and that we were more capable. As soon as the lactic acid that burns our muscles dissipates, the regret and second-guessing begins. Replaying the race I can't find an answer and so convince myself that I didn't have enough strength to close the gap. But still, my mind reels and spins.

Outside the room, thunder rolls in the distant hills. Spring storms animated the race with crashes. The peloton raced nervously on a technical and undulating course. Finishing with coal miners' faces, the photographers' cameras snapped our portraits as if we were pin-ups. This is a side of cycling we only see in their images and in the mirror after the race. The effects of the effort are felt internally: chattering teeth under a cold rain, eyes burning with road grit, aching muscles and seared lungs.

Like lightening illuminating a sky at dusk, the television images light up the cracks in the ceiling of the dim room. Neither of us watch or listen to the newscaster. The therapist focuses on my legs. Water flows in the bathroom as Igor, our mechanic, showers off the grease, sweat and grime accumulated from a day spent in the back of the team car and an evening spent washing and repairing bikes. Mechanics have a unique perspective on and perception of the race and the internal organisation of the team. From the back seat of the car, he silently observes the directeur's commands, our reactions, our heroics and our failures. A mechanic's observations are perhaps more accurate than my biased memories.

Now rubbing oily liniment into my thighs, the soigneur can feel with his hands the consequences of the effort that the photos fail to capture. An occasional bead of sweat drops from his brow. With his hands he can feel the effort the photos fail to capture. My thoughts race backwards, into my past, to previous races, where I had held on to the front group to fight for the win. Decades have now passed since the first pro races I rode: the Olympics in '96, a few European stage races and before that, when I was a teenager, the pro-amateur races in the United States. Remembering the attacks I followed in the Olympics and how I was then dropped from the lead group, I realise how I have matured. Cycling has evolved but the transition has hardened me. On the bike, my emotions are the same but the context has changed.

Half an hour before I climbed onto the massage table we were on the team bus, chatting about the race, listening to music and eating bowls of hot rice. A pile of used towels lay in the aisle between the two rows of grey, reclining leather seats. Laundry bags labelled with riders' names and filled with our dirty race clothing had been tossed in the back of the bus for the team staff to wash and return before we went to bed.

With time, error and experience, I have learned and accepted the required life; the habits and sacrifice of a professional cyclist. As a boy, I was naive about what that life involved. I emulated the professionals I saw on television and in magazines, trying to adopt their positions and style. I trained improperly, ate foolishly before key events, and wasted energy when I wasn't riding. My father taught me, and I learned from local coaches. As I progressed, so did the knowledge of my advisors. But even now, as a veteran in the peloton, I find the job is constantly evolving and we are all still learning.

The peloton now reflects the changes in the world economy, internationalisation, and cultural and social shifts. Yet it remains an insular environment. It is only understood by those who travel with the team for seasons, seeing the changes in riders, listening to their stories at mealtimes, and sharing their nomadic lives with only an emotional thread tying everyone to a home of his own.

Riders no longer look to superstition, tradition and anecdote to help their performance. Science and education have made our diets, rest, training and tactics more rational. During the 1970s and 1980s the first Americans in the peloton – Greg LeMond, Jock Boyer and the 7-Eleven team – questioned the European traditions and techniques. As mavericks, they developed and innovated. The Europeans laughed until they were beaten by the brash Americans. Then they copied. Innovation in sports science continues to be led by outsiders: Team Sky and the Australian-based GreenEDGE team have become dominant in a short period of time by using their budgets to maximise their riders' potential through analysis and innovation. Riders are attracted to these squads because they know they'll receive the support to improve and perform better.

Teams and individuals look for gains in every aspect of the sport, both mental and physical. As our manager Dave Brailsford often says: "We will leave no stone unturned." The team now analyses our food intake, weighs us daily, monitors our hydration and provides us with every legal technical advantage available. Prior generations relied on drugs to enhance performance. Today testing, negative media attention and investigation have virtually eliminated them. Teams went from doping their riders to fearing the doped as they quickly realised sponsorship could be lost with one positive test.

When I rode the Olympics in 1996 the culture of cycling was toxic. In the road race, I questioned and doubted every rider's physique and result. The negative thoughts left me sour and empty. Now I no longer question performances but accept them as genuine. Some cyclists will always cheat in an attempt to get an edge – just like some businessmen or students. But no longer do we feel pressure to dope to maintain a spot in the peloton.

During the final 15 minutes of the massage, Klaus's fingers work their way down my spine, vertebra by vertebra, sensing the sore spots and working out the tension. Igor sits on the end of the single bed with his towel around his waist. They've both worked in cycling long enough to have recognised the changes in the way we approach the sport and in the way we race.

With time, the peloton has become increasingly transparent in every respect. Photographers not only document the races but also film us in our in hotel rooms, on buses, on the street. We post our training data online, update our whereabouts for the anti-doping organisations, tweet about where we've ridden, and upload photos of those rides on Facebook. No longer do we wait for the results of the day to be delivered to the hotel in the evening; they are downloaded from the internet as we sit on the team bus, still sweating from the effort. Minutes after the finish, we report what happened in the race to our families and friends over our mobile phones.

As a boy, I would have spent every idle moment devouring the information that is available to fans today. The peloton has become globally accessible. But that constant flow of information emanating from the races and teams has also changed the attitude of the riders who feature in it. With our egos constantly fed, we elevate our self-worth. Each of us becomes a superstar in his own small galaxy. The cascade of attention turns common occurrences into events while also eroding our small community.

Throughout the massage, Klaus's mobile phone has buzzed and chimed. He hasn't moved his hands from my body to answer. Now, as I climb down from the table, he towels the oil from his hands and begins to look through the messages. I return to the room where my room-mate Mat Hayman chats with his wife online.

We sit in similar positions on our single beds and I poke at my phone while I wait for him to finish the conversation. He is a veteran in the peloton, and I want to ask him how he thinks it has changed. Other than the names that are stickered to the outside of the Samsonites, there is little to distinguish our two suitcases sitting open in either corner of the room. They're filled with identical branded clothing, equally as upturned.

Although I'm slightly older than Mat, we've raced together and against each other for over a decade. As fathers, we share stories about our boys who wait at home while our wives count the days until our return. Cycling has brought us both to Europe, transplanting our families. As foreigners in Europe, we are part of the internationalisation of cycling.

Fourteen years ago, I spoke more French than English within the peloton. The English-speaking riders would seek each other out as we were all starving for conversation in our native language. With the steady influx of North Americans, Eastern Europeans, Asians, and Africans into the peloton, cycling's common language has become English. A Spanish rider will converse in English with a Dutch team-mate. An Italian will tweet to his international fans in English. A once European sport has become global on every level.

The peloton now travels across continents to races almost throughout the year. The off season is rapidly shortening as we move to the southern hemisphere from October through to February and race in the warmth of their summer. The gaps between races are filled with training camps to ensure we are fit and ready to accumulate victories and points. Events in

China, Australia, Canada and the United States are replacing the European races, which struggle to survive due to a suffering economy and increasingly congested roads.

The internationalisation has raised the level of competition. Drawing from a larger pool of athletes, the peloton is now more competitive and the differences in riders' abilities have diminished. With larger budgets, teams have more resources. Equipment is light, aerodynamic and stiff. Training is more scientific and riders race in near-peak condition year round. Race tactics are dictated by the directeurs over radios. The increased momentum of the peloton has levelled the courses and we now barrel over climbs that once splintered the groups. Massive group sprints are too common. The racing up until the final kilometres often becomes controlled and mundane. To compensate, race organisers have introduced more climbs and dangerously technical sections in the final kilometres. For the riders this only increases the level of anxiety.

The pressure to perform is constant. For 10 months of the year, teams chase points to qualify in the rankings for the following season. If a team fails, it risks losing a sponsor. In a faltering global economy, advertising budgets are constrained so we fight for every piece of attention. Each kilometre of a race has value.

As these changes continue, riders' careers will no longer last 15 years. Injuries from crashes and overuse will become increasingly common. With a larger pool of athletes and few long-term contracts, teams will constantly seek out fresh talent, changing their rosters with greater frequency. It is a trend that has already happened in most other professional sports. The star players endure while the team-mates who surround them are discarded.

Mat says a quick goodbye to his wife. In the conversation he has recounted his perspective of the race; a race that she has followed online from another perspective. I put down my phone and ask him how he thinks the peloton has changed.

Mat is a Classics rider who excels on the cobbles of northern Europe. He's also a powerful domestique who positions the team sprinter for his final charge to the finish line. These are the two most dangerous jobs in cycling. The riders who spearhead the peloton as it speeds towards the finish in a tight mass are skilled at handling their bicycles and in sensing the movements of the other riders. They ride with a heightened level of respect for each other to ensure the safety of the whole. They dodge parked cars and brush signposts, hop curbs, and jump over traffic islands. They repeatedly knock shoulders with other riders, clip pedals, and buzz each other's tyres.

The official race rules don't include the unwritten agreement adhered to by the riders to keep the peloton safe. The commissaries only refer to the rule book in extreme cases, when a rider deviates significantly from his line and puts his co-workers at risk. Within the charging mass, one rider can kill another in an instant if he doesn't consider his movements and position on the road. In the last 20 years, the riders' attitude and etiquette in the final charge has progressively deteriorated. The hope of victory often eclipses their fear.

Sadly the loss of respect is not unique to the finale. No longer do we slow down when a crash occurs to allow the fallen riders to return to the bunch. Far too often, the peloton accelerates as the skids, cracks and screams of falling cyclists fill the air. Those who have avoided the crash see it as an opportunity to gain an advantage. José Azevedo, an ex-team-mate of mine who now works as a directeur sportif, commented on the change after one of his riders crashed: "What's happening with cycling?" he said. "After only five kilometres of racing there was a massive crash. Normally the peloton would wait for everyone to get back on the bikes. Not any more. There was no waiting. It's a war out there every day and there is no solidarity. It's unbelievable."

Children now grow up watching extreme sports on television and idolise those athletes. While extreme sports attract an audience, there is an innate flaw that will make them unsustainable – their athletes must constantly go higher and faster to satisfy the fans. Each Olympic cycle introduces an unsettling number of extreme sports to increase television viewership. Society has embraced the extreme, but it comes at the expense of a healthy future for the athletes. Sometimes it comes at the expense of their lives. Like gladiators in Roman times, athletes have become expendable. Cycling isn't immune to this trend. Riders now take less responsibility for their actions. Slowly we are becoming numb to risk.

In the 2012 Giro d'Italia, Mark Cavendish – the world champion, and my team-mate – came crashing down at over 75 km/h when Roberto Ferrari, a fairly unknown young sprinter, wildly deviated from his racing line. Ferrari's erratic move across the road brought down Cavendish, and a dozen other riders then piled into him. Covered in scrapes, cuts and bruises, Cavendish walked across the finish line with his bicycle on his shoulder. Ferrari crossed the line unfazed by his actions and the damage he caused. When asked about the crash he said that he can't see what happens behind him and doesn't care.

The respect among riders, the etiquette in the peloton, is what gives us our solidarity. The experience of travelling together for thousands of kilometres through arduous and thrilling conditions creates a bond. The shared life transcends culture and age. We are rivals but also colleagues. To maintain the intrigue and competitiveness of the sport without excessive danger and ruthlessness, riders need to regard each other with solidarity and respect. Yet we are losing our unity.

On the VeloNews website, Cavendish was quoted as saying: "Things are changing in the peloton. There's not the respect there used to be and that means there are a lot more crashes. I have been a student of the sport. Things are changing in the sport as a whole. I am not sitting here saying we have to go back. I am not saying if it's right or wrong, there is just less respect in the peloton."

Of course, fearlessness has always affected racing. The cyclist is required to push the boundaries of his comfort; to reach his physical and mental limit but without endangering the safety of his co-workers. Those limits are policed internally within the group. Over the last 15 years, however, fewer riders have been willing to police others for the safety of the whole. Past generations understood that their futures and their families depended on the money made through racing. Now that understanding seems less apparent.

During a long drive home after a race, I had a discussion about the shift in mentality with our team mechanic David Fernandez, a Catalan who has worked in cycling since he was a boy. He witnessed the evolution of ONCE and Banesto, the dominant Spanish teams for two decades. A generation ago, the best teams would develop their young riders. The development was not only an apprenticeship but also a schooling. The teams invested in the rider's physical strengths and worked to develop respect and etiquette, both in the peloton and at the dinner table. Young riders matured in the team's culture until they developed into champions. At mealtimes, their friendship and bonds were evident and carried over into the races where they worked and sacrificed for the common goal. Nowadays, riders scurry up to their rooms soon after they finish eating to log on, check in, or tune out. Fewer sit around enjoying each other's company while waiting for a team-mate to finish his meal. Too often that team-mate now sits alone while waiters clear the places around him.

Building a strong team requires a vigilant directeur who, like a teacher, keeps his distance from the riders so that he can reprimand and command respect. Christian Rumeau once told me the greatest error a directeur can make is to become friends with the riders.

Fewer directeurs now teach or lead with this authority. Within most teams it is now the general managers who command and the coaches who advise. The directeurs have become middlemen. The managers – who are less frequently at the races and more often at the office or courting sponsors – don't have the same rapport with the riders as directeurs do. They aren't with us daily to observe our personalities, our conflicts, and our strengths. The lopsided leadership creates an imbalance; individual results often outweigh the work done for the team, on and off the road.

The riders who animate the team at the dinner table or on the bus, who work tirelessly on the road but who finish at the back once their work is complete, are often the pillars of the team. But they no longer have the same value on a team as a domestique did a decade ago. Now, often to the detriment of the team as a whole, riders chase results and points to increase their own value. They know that those results are more marketable than a job well done.

Mat and I clean up and head down for dinner. Some of our team-mates are already at the table, tucking into mountains of pasta. They are young and confident Brits, at home within Team Sky. Although my career has been an exhilarating journey, I am slightly jealous of them. They are beginning their careers in a time of transition, when anything is possible. They belong to an English-speaking team, which will support them to achieve their best as long as they maintain their work ethic. In a cleaner peloton their natural achievements will be pronounced. Yet it will also be their responsibility to ensure their workplace is considerate and safe.

Cycling's rapid evolution is thrilling to witness. While alone in a hotel in small European hamlet I'm aware of the fans following the race in Canada and around the world. Through our actions millions of people will be inspired to ride their bicycles, which is ultimately the greatest reason to race.

The growth of cycling is stunning. City centres are being forced to adapt their infrastructures to accommodate swarms of cycling commuters. Although racing in Europe is struggling, the sport is growing internationally. Races in Canada, Australia and the United States draw massive crowds of spectators. If it is properly governed, managed and policed, professional cycling can grow to become a top tier international sport, like tennis, football, golf or Formula 1. Riders are as responsible for the future as the governing bodies are. Often we, the riders, think we are impotent within the structure but our voice can and should be the strongest. The race is our job, our life and our future.

Michael returns from the finish in Arosa. Tour de Suisse. 2012.

Dead man walking

Thomas Löfkvist on the table

Glaubenberg Pass, Tour de Suisse, 2010

Morning transfer from hotel to start

The team bus cannot reach the hotel. Team cars are used instead for transfers

Hotel Alpina, Arosa. Tour de Suisse 2012.

OVERLEAF: The authors. Mount Pleasant Cemetery, Toronto 1982.